2013

5

4/9/12

Ple

Y

CUSTOMER SERVICE EXCELLEN

No Smoke,
No Fire

No Smoke, No Fire

The Autobiography of
DAVE JONES

© Dave Jones and Andrew Warshaw, 2009

The right of Dave Jones and Andrew Warshaw to be identified as the authors of this work has been asserted by them in accordance with sections 77 and 78 of the Copyright, Designs and Patents Act, 1988.

Know The Score Books Limited
118 Alcester Road
Studley
Warwickshire
B80 7NT
01527 454482
info@knowthescorebooks.com
www.knowthescorebooks.com

A CIP catalogue record is available for this book from the British Library
ISBN: 978-1-84818-513-5

Printed and bound in Poland
By

ACKNOWLEDGEMENTS

My thanks go to Andrew Warshaw, without whom this book would not have been possible. His assiduous work and pursuit of the truth, honesty and accuracy have allowed me to tell my story in exactly the way in which I wanted.

Thanks as well to Simon Lowe and all his staff at Know The Score Books, especially Richard Roper, Tony Lyons and Gareth Stringer, and Richard Munden at 5rb. Graham Hales has also been an invaluable help throughout the whole process of the production of the book.

Of course everyone who has helped me in any way throughout my career with all of my clubs has to have a big thank you. There are so many so I won't attempt to name you all, but you know who you are and I couldn't have done any of it without you.

I owe a huge debt of gratitude to the thousands of well-wishers and to my close friends especially Phil and Jenny Jones, Dina and John Nixon, Joanne O'Neil, Jeff and Ian, Tommy Cawley, Neil Lofthouse, Chris and John Sainty, Stuart and Kath Gray, Dennis and Sue Rofe, Mr and Mrs Gordon. In addition, a huge thanks to my legal team – Henry Globe, Stephen Pollard, Linzi McDonald and all at Kingsley Napley – plus my many colleagues in the football industry who supported me throughout the torrid ordeal which I was subjected to. You will read about many of them in these pages but there were so many who offered assistance and support I can't possibly name them all. You know who you are and a little piece of my heart goes out to all of you.

Finally all my love to Ann and our wonderful children Lea, Danielle, Chloe and Georgia. Also to my grandchildren Luca, Maddison and Taylor and of course to my beloved mum, brothers Billy and Mark, sister Tracey and their respective families. An enormous tribute must also go to Ann's family including Dot, Linda, Pauline, Philip, Brian and John – and their families. Last but by no means least, I also dedicate this book to my late dad and Ann's late parents. Without you all, none of this would have been worth the fight.

Dave Jones
May 2009

CONTENTS

FOREWORD BY
BILL KENWRIGHT

I remember it as if it were yesterday. February 1st 1977. A freezing cold night at Goodison Park for a fourth round FA Cup replay against Swindon Town. With the scores tied at 1-1 and just a few minutes remaining, it looked like it was going to be a repeat of the score draw the previous Saturday. Then, right in front of me on Everton's defensive side of the halfway line, our full-back Dave Jones picked up the ball. He ran, and ran, and ran – avoiding tackles, avoiding bodies, and eventually slamming the ball into the back of the Swindon net for the winner. I can remember sitting there not quite believing what I had just seen! Our already tall full-back had suddenly grown into a Colossus in front of the Goodison faithful!

I had always liked him enormously as a player. He was young, sometimes raw, and even naïve – but he displayed an enthusiasm and a passion that simply led you to believe that you were watching a real footballer.

That was 1977 and now, 32 years later, I still believe in Dave Jones – as a footballer, as a manager and, most importantly, as a man. The years may have stripped away the youth and the naïvety, but Dave remains a passionate and driven individual. He has needed all of that passion and drive – and a lot more – over the last decade or so.

In all of the games that I watched Dave play for Everton I can honestly say that I never saw him shirk a tackle. He was never afraid to go in where it hurt. An uncompromising full-back who, after almost committing the cardinal sin of joining Liverpool, successfully worked his way through the invariably crowded ranks at Everton back in the days when tackles were tackles and wingers were scared.

Ironically, it was a bad tackle which was to move him towards early retirement. He had left his beloved Everton by that point and was playing in a reserve game for Coventry City against Derby County when he sustained a knee injury which was to ruin his career and change his life. He was upset by it, of course he was, but, typical of the man, he has never felt moved to name the other player involved.

Dave's move forward into management was almost inevitable – he's a Scouser, and just like rubber balls, they will bounce back at you. As one door was slammed shut in his face, he kicked another one open with his good leg! Proving himself to be a manager players could not only relate to but respect, he almost did the impossible by taking Stockport County to a League Cup semi-final and so nearly to Wembley, and achieved what so many Wolves fans believed WAS, indeed, impossible by returning them to the Premiership after an absence of 19 years.

I saw him on a couple of occasions at Southampton, where he seemed to be worshipped by a fan base that I have always believed to be one of the fairest in the country. What happened to Dave while he was at Southampton will obviously form a part of this book – suffice to say, I couldn't understand it, and to this day I still don't. At the precise moment his managerial career seemed destined to bring him the success that his footballing days had probably not, he was confronted by the sort of lurid accusations – and accompanying tabloid headlines – that would have broken a lesser man. But faced by the very real prospect of both public condemnation and professional ruin, Dave simply reverted to type, displaying the sort of calm dignity and enviable stoicism which not only sets him apart from most, but which makes him a special man.

He didn't shirk the tackles, he stood proud on the defensive side of the half-way line and took on every single body that was thrown at him.

I don't know how he did it on that freezing cold night in February and, even more so, I don't know how he did it during those horrible, horrible months that he and his family had to live through.

But he did. And he won.

He survived the cruel and wholly false allegations of those with malice in their hearts not simply because he is mentally and emotionally strong, but because above all else he is an honest man and a decent man.

As I pen these notes, Dave Jones and Cardiff City have just missed out on a chance of promotion to the Premier League elite by the cruellest margin possible – just one goal. I texted Dave only hours after what must have been a real moment of despair for him – just as I had contacted him several years before as he walked into that court room to wish him well. His response was typical. "Thank you, I will come out fighting". And he will Cardiff City fans! He doesn't know any other way. He gives his best – all the time – whatever the occasion. I am sure you are proud of him. I am.

Dave's text back to me after Cardiff's heartbreak went on to say, 'Well done today' – Everton had beaten Sunderland in an away game only two hours after Cardiff City had been dealt their cruel blow. He took the time to remember.

Dave – Respect, my friend!

Bill Kenwright

PROLOGUE

15 June 1999

THE DOOR OF the police interview room clanked shut.

I was alone. The place was dank and windowless, smelt like a hospital ward and paint peeled off its walls.

I knew there was something badly wrong. The two police officers who had been grilling me had left me in this hellhole to go and discuss something they didn't want me to hear.

It couldn't be good.

I knew this was some sort of game the police were trying to play with me, but I couldn't quite understand why. Operation Care, the investigation into child abuse in Merseyside children's care homes, had been running for a long time now and I had been asked several times before to dredge my memory for anything I could think of that could help the police with their enquiries. But on this occasion everything felt different.

I tried to idle away some time by thinking about my Southampton squad, its strengths and weaknesses, and the coming 1999/2000 campaign.

My thoughts also drifted back to the fun times I'd had at Clarence House, working with the underprivileged kids who came from backgrounds far less fortunate than mine. I had certainly never seen or heard of any abuse taking place and I'd told the police so before.

The door opened and banged against the wall, jolting me from my thoughts. Then it creaked shut again, closing out the daylight from the corridor outside. The two officers had returned. One walked straight up to the table behind which I was sitting and leaned over, his eyes boring into me, seeking something deep inside me which he thought he would find, but I knew he couldn't – guilt.

He spoke, but the words were somehow incomprehensible, yet at the same time as dark and threatening as the room I now felt a prisoner in.

"David Jones, you are under arrest."

I felt my stomach lurch, the lights burn into my widening eyes and my skin start to crawl.

"Arrest? What for?" I managed to force myself to ask.

"Physical abuse and . . . (I remember the second part of the sentence as if he said the words in slow motion) . . . sexual abuse of minors."

'Hold on a minute,' I thought as my mind computed the context of what this meant. They are arresting me for being a paedophile. That's what sexual abuse of children means.

In that split second I felt the whole room collapse on top of me. Everything was shutting down and I was floating above myself watching what was happening. Every single thing around me was a blur, yet I could clearly see myself sitting there, angry and confused. At the same time I could hear a voice pounding inside my head shouting 'this is not real'.

And yet it was. All too real. I was being accused of the most horrendous crime imaginable. The police officer's words cut like a knife through my heart. I felt like they had accused me of being the Ripper.

Without thinking further I blurted out, "Someone is falsely accusing me of being a paedophile and you are actually believing them? This cannot be happening and it has to stop. Right now."

And then the questions began swirling in my head. How do I tell Ann? How do I tell my parents? How do I tell my kids? And what on earth would this mean for my job as manager of Southampton Football Club, a position I had battled so hard to earn?

Then the biggest question of all struck fear into my heart and I felt physically sick . . . what if I could not prove my utter innocence? What then?

FOOTBALL ON MY MIND

AS FAR BACK as I can remember, I have lived and breathed football – schools football, boys' club football, professional football, my first big break coming when Liverpool FC spotted me playing in the local youth league as a 14-year-old and asked me to go and train with them – even though I was a staunch Everton fan, a Blue nose!

Football was always a topic of conversation in our close-knit household comprising mum Pat, dad Bill, sister Tracey and my two brothers. Mum always joked I'd sleepwalk in my boots and that was at the age of five! I can't remember a time when I wasn't totally obsessed by the game and we used to play in the house – me, Billy and our Mark – which drove mum potty. Even after she'd confiscated all our balls, we'd blow up a balloon and kick it around the house until she screamed at us to stop.

There are two particular stories my mum loves to recall about how young I was when I demonstrated my passion for the game. One Christmas Eve mum and dad had finally got four excitable kids to sleep and had just dropped off themselves around two in the morning when they heard noises downstairs as though someone was trying to break in and steal the presents. Dad sat bolt upright and listened. Then he got out of bed and crept downstairs, followed by mum, to confront the interloper. All they could hear was this sound coming from the front door. They expected to discover a thief, instead of which they found I had unwrapped everything and was standing at the door in my new Everton kit, trying to get out of the house to kick my new football about. I had somehow even managed to lace up my boots in the pitch black and as mum and dad switched the lights on, ready to pounce on whoever it was, I had finally managed to get the front door open and was just about to step outside into the pitch black.

There was another incident, not so long afterwards, when this friend of the family called up my parents to say that "David is at the bottom of the road wearing shinpads." Mum said that wasn't possible since I didn't have any shinpads. Guess what I had done? Only gone and pinched a couple of my mum's sanitary towels from her bathroom, hooked them round my legs and tied them to my socks with sticky tape! When mum tells that story now I like to claim that it was a way of improvising and thinking on my feet which I have taken all through my life in football.

We didn't have a great deal of money, but we were by no means poverty stricken and my parents made the best of what they had. My dad, who I worshipped, took me everywhere in the car even before it became clear that I was going to make it in the game. We used to watch Everton together on the terraces, me standing on one of those makeshift wooden crates kids used to use to crane their necks to get a decent view. I especially remember the first game I went to on my own, or at least with my mates rather than my dad. I must have been about 12 at the time and the thrill of boarding the train, getting off the other end and watching from the terraces at Blackpool was indescribable. If I am not mistaken, I never told mum and dad. They'd have gone mad if they knew I'd gone off to an away game with friends!

Like so many households in the area, we were both red and blue. One of my brothers was red – still is. The banter was often hilarious and I still recall one incident that always has me in stitches. It was my first derby match as a player and as I stepped off the team coach at Anfield, my uncle Don, who was a local policeman and a staunch Liverpool fan, played a trick on me. As I started to walk into the ground, two bobbies strode up alongside me, told me they were arresting me, frogmarched me into a the side-room and finger-printed me.

"David Jones," they said, though they could barely keep a straight face, "we are arresting you for being an Evertonian!" My uncle, of course, thought it was hilarious. I kind of knew it was a wind-up, but it was typical of the friendly rivalry in those days. You could travel to derby games and one side of the car would be red, the other blue. There was no animosity or anger because in the car were mums and dads, brothers and sisters, uncles and aunts. It brought a whole new meaning to the phrase 'mixed marriages'!

My older brother Billy always enjoyed kicking a ball around, but never played seriously. The younger one, Mark, followed in my footsteps and became a professional, though he never quite reached the same level as me, moving into non-league football after a stint with Preston North End. These days, Billy still works in the same factory in Widnes where he has been since leaving school at 15 years of age, while Mark is an assessor for children with behavioural problems and Tracey is a school secretary.

Dad was an accountant with a firm named Martindale and Carlisle, a company that specialised in two different areas, coal yards, and car sales and garages. I know accountant sounds middle-class, but we really weren't, even though Ann and I have always joked about the fact that when she had Stork margarine as a kid, we had butter. Yes we were a bit better off than my wife's family were, but mum had to work as a cleaner to pay the bills. She may not like me saying it, but we were always told not to open the door to strangers as it might be the debt collector. Having said all that, I never felt we wanted for anything – we were well fed and well clothed – but dad worked hard for it and we never asked for anything either – except new football boots.

We lived in an old three-bedroom terraced house in Toxteth in which I shared a room with Billy. Even though Toxteth came to be notorious for rioting in the early 1980s, there was no trouble – or at least I never witnessed it – when we lived there. Everyone was your auntie or your uncle, metaphorically speaking. You never locked your door and could just walk into people's houses to say 'hello'. That was through the 1960s. About three years ago we actually took our youngest daughter, Georgia, to see the house I grew up in. It was a really warm Sunday, but she was absolutely astounded to see everyone barbecuing in the street. There are no gardens still, so people were just sitting out on sun chairs. Georgia's face was agog. She had never seen anything like that, nor have any of my children, who have grown up in a very different era and in very different surroundings. To me, back then, it was the norm.

My nan and grandad lived in the next street. Everyone knew everyone, I wouldn't be surprised if I bumped into Ann at some point without knowing who she was. It was a really close community. So close, would you believe, that the same doctor who delivered me delivered my future wife too.

Even when we moved to a new estate at Halewood on the outskirts of the city – I was around ten at that point – I still shared a room with Billy, who was four years older than me. Sharing wasn't that bad because when our Billy used to go out, I'd pinch his shoes or some of his clothes and hide them in the cubby hole outside the house so he wouldn't find out. He'd have killed me if he knew. I was still at school and he was working, so he had far nicer clothes. Sometimes he knew I'd been wearing his shoes because I had bigger feet and used to stretch them. He went absolutely mad and there were heated arguments as I used to totally deny it.

My decision to make a career out of professional football wasn't universally accepted at my school, Halewood Grange, which, these days, is right next to Everton's new state-of-the-art training ground. I remember the careers officer, Mr. Champion, who was also head of sports, clipping me round the ear and saying "don't be stupid, son, come into the real world." Funnily enough, when I got into Everton's first team a couple of years later and went back to the school to make a presentation I brought that up and told the kids that if they had a dream not to let anything get in its way and to have a go. Mr Champion was still there and, to be fair, could see the funny side.

When I left school, dad got me a job as a car mechanic with his firm which meant working at one of the garages and going to college to do my apprenticeship – except that I never actually went to any of the lectures. Instead, I got the books from a mate of mine and did all the work from home. My dad would have gone bananas if he'd ever found out. After all, he'd worked so hard to set me up in a job in the first place. But football was in my blood by this time and nothing could get in the way. As well as playing for my school and Woolton boys club – where I also played table tennis and snooker, as you did in them days – I also played for our Billy's Sunday team. Now that really hardened me up as I was playing in a man's team. The rest of the players were all four years older than me. I had to pretend I was over-16, even though I was actually only 12.

It was while I was playing for Woolton boys club that I got picked up by Liverpool and asked to train with them. I had played basketball, rugby, cricket and hockey as a kid, but this was what I had always wanted – even if it was for the other lot. Suddenly Tuesday and Thursday nights meant only one thing – and it wasn't being at college learning about car engines. It was fantastic to be associated with Liverpool, but it soon became apparent there was a problem. I couldn't get into their county schoolboys team because, after taking a look at me in the training sessions, they didn't think I was good enough to go on and have a professional career. Perhaps, looking back, that was fortuitous as it was what caused my boyhood dream to start to take shape.

One day when I was playing for Woolton an elderly gentleman named Tommy Ferfowl came to watch. Afterwards he asked me if I'd like to train with Everton, for whom he was scouting. I told him this wasn't possible since I was already training with Liverpool.

"Are you an Evertonian?" he asked. When I replied that indeed I was, he was pretty direct. "Then you are coming to Everton." I wasn't going to turn that down, now was I?

These days I guess it would constitute tapping up, but I hadn't signed anything at Liverpool – except my expense forms. Tuesdays and Thursday evenings carried on, but now it was very much on Blue-nose territory, although my parents still didn't know.

During this time I guess I could easily have neglected my studies. Actually I did to be honest, though I still managed to do enough to pass my City and Guilds mechanics exam. Don't ask me how. Maybe it's because the mechanics I worked under during the day gave me so many jobs to do, teaching me in-house. I guess I took to it like a duck to water because after about six months I knew how to service vehicles. I even learned to drive at 15, which was amusing because when I eventually took my driving test two years later, I didn't have a single lesson. I just turned up and passed.

That meant being legally allowed to drive my first car, a bright yellow Ford Escort which I had already bought, but wasn't allowed – officially at least – to use. My future wife Ann hated the colour with a vengeance and thought my family were all posh because hers never had a car and we had two.

Training with Everton was sheer bliss. After all, I had been watching them as a kid and can still reel off the names of that great side. Gordon West in goal, Tommy Wright and Sandy Brown at full-back, Brian Labone and John Hurst in central defence; a midfield of Ball, Harvey and Kendall, all of them heroes of mine; Jimmy Husband on one wing, Alan Whittle over on the left, and Joe Royle down the middle. I'd play for my school in the morning, then go and watch the Toffees in the afternoon. What could be better?

Nothing for me. I actually got offered trials at rugby league, and to be a kicker in American Football. One of the earliest teams to come across from the States – I can't remember which one – used Everton's training ground at Bellfield one day during their visit and saw me, a mere schoolboy player, messing around. They were agog I could kick balls so far and I was told that if I ever wanted to make a career in America, I'd walk it. Was I tempted? No, because I was playing with my heroes, blue through and through.

I was in my element at Everton playing in the youth team, living out the dream I shared with half of Merseyside. But that all changed on 7 April 1973 when the manager at the time, the legendary Harry Catterick, got the sack. Harry, a former Everton player, had led the club through the glory years of the 1960s, but, despite having four years still left on his contract at that point, health problems, including a heart attack 14 months previously, left the board feeling they needed a fitter, more capable man to do the job. Harry was relieved of his duties. The fallout had immediate repercussions for me. That same day I was told I wasn't needed any more.

Catterick, renowned for being an authoritarian manager, was one of those figures you were in awe of – particularly if you were as young as me. I had only been there a few months and hadn't had too many dealings with him, but I remember him walking down the tunnel at the training ground one day and saying "good afternoon" to me.

"Good afternoon," I duly replied. He stopped me in my tracks, paused and admonished me: "Good afternoon . . . boss" before walking on.

I must have been about 15 at the time and it was a rare moment in front of the great man, who'd led Everton to two league titles and an FA Cup triumph while I was growing up.

I was totally devastated when told I was surplus to requirements aged 16½, but even then I was something of a stubborn bugger and wasn't going to let it deter me. You can't let stuff like that affect you if you're going to make a success in football, or indeed in life. As it happened, over that single weekend all the coaching staff got the boot along with Catterick, so I thought I'd just turn up again on the following Tuesday and chance my arm to see if anyone knew I'd been released. No-one was any the wiser. It was as if nothing had happened!

I quickly came under the wing of a former centre-half called Tommy G. Jones, who used to hand out the expenses for the bus fare home to us kids. Tommy, in his day, had been a well-known Everton player, a member of the League title-winning team of 1938/39, and under his guidance I watched as many home games as I could. That was how you got educated in those days – you went and watched your seniors. It was great sitting with an old-timer like Tommy, picking up tips on how to mark, when to time tackles, when to stand off. He got me thinking about my game, and I learnt that, despite what many people might think, being a defender, particularly in the central position, is about using your brains, in a footballing sense, to outplay your direct opponent.

Who knows what might have transpired had I obeyed orders and stayed away. Maybe I'd have ended up in the navy as a marine. It was certainly something I had long considered if I never made the grade in football. At one point I actually went to a careers office to find out more, though I never told mum and dad about it. They'd have gone barmy at the thought of it. But to me it seemed a good life, travelling the world and all that. But once football had got hold of me, I never looked back.

Not that the college I was supposed to attend were very pleased. They backchecked all the records and finally discovered that I hadn't been going. Who was this guy who had passed an exam without having actually attended? They called the company I worked for, who took the necessary action – which I still think was a bit harsh as I'd actually passed the exam, despite my non-existent attendance record – and I had to go home and tell dad that I'd been sacked. He was angry because it was hard to get jobs in those days, but luckily Everton asked me to go in and sign semi-professional forms. So now I was picking up £7 a week for expenses and it seemed my future lay in football if I could make the grade. Although I had been earning slightly more as a car mechanic, it was the opportunity I had always craved. On my 17th birthday, in August 1973, it got even better when they called me in to sign pro.

For some reason I thought I was going to getting released that day when I was summoned to the office. I can't explain why, I'd just got it into my head. Maybe it was because I thought some who were getting released were better than me. You just got the feeling the club were having a bit of a cull. When they told me about the pro contract I couldn't believe it. The feeling was euphoric – all that hard work and dad taking me everywhere, dropping me off at training, always driving out of his way – it all suddenly seemed worthwhile. The first thing I did was call dad to say I had some news for him, but I didn't tell him what it was on the phone. I broke the news when we met at the local chippy and we celebrated with a bag of chips before going home to tell the rest of the family.

Perhaps, looking back, I should have twigged that Everton would take me on because there was an occasion when I was playing for the under-18 side and got substituted at half-time. I was really angry because I thought I was doing okay in the game. In fact what had happened is that the centre-half for the reserves had got injured and they wanted me to replace him for a game at Old Trafford. I ended up lining up alongside the likes of Howard Kendall, Colin Harvey and Joe Royle. It was mind-blowing playing with people whose boots I had been cleaning only 12 months earlier. In fact the senior pros were brilliant to us youngsters. For example Colin Harvey used to pick me up and take me to training, even though he lived 40 minutes away from us. What a gentleman. Can you imagine that happening today?

Let me tell you how I first met Joe Royle. When I was starting to show promise as an apprentice with Everton, Eric Harrison, who famously went on to scout for Manchester United and unearth such gems as David Beckham, the Neville brothers and Paul Scholes, was my youth coach. Everton were so good in those days that they put a C team of 15 and 16 year-olds in the local adult Sunday league, including me. It was unheard of and literally men against boys, but it was a fantastic education for me. We used to get battered from pillar to post, maybe not in terms of the score but physically. It certainly toughened us up, which, as I found to my cost, was very necessary. Every day in training, Joe, who would have been in his late 20s, used to practise his finishing against the young centre-halves at the club. Eric Harrison jibed him there was young defender (me) with promise, who would make life difficult for him. I was called over to give Joe some stiff opposition. It went well, as I beat Big Joe to headers, got in some well-timed tackles and generally made a nuisance of myself. So there I was, getting to the ball before Joe and thinking to myself, 'that Joe Royle's not so good as I thought he was,' when, all of a sudden, I feel a crashing pain in my head and my nose is all over my face. Blood streaming. Joe had flung an elbow at me. "Hey son," he said, "you want to watch these big, hairy-arsed centre-forwards doing that to you."

I waited four years for my revenge. In 1979 I was playing for Everton's first team and Joe was playing for Norwich. I went right through the back of him with a tough tackle and he turned and asked me what the hell I was doing. "You need to watch these young hairy-arsed centre-halves," I said. Point made. . .

When I started out, clubs the size of Everton had 50-odd pros and the reserves were almost as good as the first team, so playing with and against them stood me in good stead for when I made my full debut aged 17. There were four different changing rooms at Goodison Park, from the first team downwards, and, being so young, I was one of the few who went straight from dressing room four, where the youth team changed, to number one with the first teamers. It was a nerve-wracking experience. I remember being told by Gordon West that if I had something to say, like "good morning", they would let me talk, but otherwise to keep quiet.

I was in awe of the lot of them, but had already done my cause no harm, having been called into the England youth set-up, along with players who would go on to become household names like West Brom's Bryan Robson, Spurs' Glenn Hoddle, Manchester City's Peter Barnes, West Ham's Alan Curbishley and Chelsea's Ray Wilkins. That was a cracking side – we used to go to places like Aston Villa and beat their first team in practice matches. I'm still friendly with a lot of them, many of whom, of course, have gone on to long careers in management and are still involved in the game today. Well I say friendly. Football is a strange environment; you might not have seen someone for years and you can literally sit down and get into a conversation as if it were yesterday. We all have so many similar experiences in common.

So by 1976, aged 20, I was becoming a regular in the Everton first team playing either centre-half or right-back, having been signed as a pro by new manager Billy Bingham, who had been a member of the 1962/63 League title-winning Everton side. The former Northern Ireland international winger had a nickname I'd rather not reveal because I had a lot of time for him. Put it this way: it was a play on words on his surname. For some reason the senior players didn't really get on with him, but I have nothing but good things to say about Billy. After all, he gave me my first contract, promoted me to the reserves in 1973 and pretty much straight away gave me my first team chance. And he got me a club house near the training ground. That was because Billy knew me and Ann were getting married. I was living in a council house at the time and he said to me, "We can't have an Everton player living in a council house," so the club sold me one of theirs for £7,500. They gave me a £500 deposit and I got a mortgage for the rest. The Everton staff were very keen for us kids to settle down because they worried about us turning into big-headed tearaways. They used to tell us if we didn't settle down we'd die of one of two things: either syphilis or wrapping a car round a tree.

THE LOVE OF MY LIFE

I'VE KNOWN ANN since our school days. I probably first clapped eyes on her at the age of 14, but I had no idea then that I wanted to be with her and to suggest it was love at first sight is a bit strong. Ann was the blonde bombshell of Halewood Grange School, so she was certainly someone I was aware of, although I was so dedicated to football that I had little time for the fairer sex. We used to both walk to school in a group of friends together and – she maybe wouldn't agree with this – it was a major feather in my cap for me to pull her. She'd probably say the same about me (I'm joking, of course!) as I was something of an all-round sportsman at school.

Mind you sport nearly put paid to any thoughts we may have had of any kind of relationship as one of my earliest memories of Ann isn't remotely romantic. It is actually the day I broke her nose! Let me explain before you get the wrong idea. There was a big indoor sports gym at school and she was in goal during an impromptu game we were playing with mixed teams. I was running through, not thinking about anything other than scoring. I got about ten yards out and shot as hard as I could. Being pretty competitive herself, Ann dived to save the ball and misjudged it, ending up getting it smack in the face. The impact smashed her nose quite badly. It wasn't a pretty sight and I still take the Mickey out of her about it to this day!

Ann was great about the whole thing. In fact we've never argued, except over the kids. Even at the height of the stress over the child abuse case, there has never been a single time where we have ever thought about calling it a day. If you put us on a scale of one to ten – ten being close to getting a divorce – we have never gone past one. Many people might wonder why what happened to me never weakened our relationship. I'll tell you why now. Ann knows me. Knows me inside out. Sometimes, I think, better than I know myself. Had there been any doubt at all, the marriage would probably have finished the day I was charged and hung out to dry before the cameras, but Ann instinctively knew I could not have done anything approaching what I was being accused of. Strangely, I feel now that it actually somehow brought us closer together. Adversity strengthens any great team.

As with any teenage lad I went out with a few girls at school, although nothing was ever particularly serious, so our first time together wasn't very long and fizzled out in our final year at school. From then I didn't see Ann for at least a year as I was working in the garage and training in the evenings. She went to work as a typist in Liverpool and when we actually got back together properly it was a blind date. Well at least blind for me because I think she secretly knew who was coming as we'd been set up by a friend of mine who knew we still carried a torch for each other.

We went to the Elephant pub in Woolton and I'll always remember what she was wearing: yellow top and yellow trousers: interesting choice given that she hated the colour of my first car. She looked absolutely stunning and from that moment we never parted. Within two years we were married. I was 19, Ann 20 and Billy, my brother, was my best man.

When we got engaged, mum and dad weren't too happy at the thought of us marrying so young. They thought it was too soon and would ruin my career. I know a lot of people split up these days, but a lot of people I know from when I started out are still with their wives. Maybe that's a generational thing across the board, but for us as a couple we simply love each other more than words can possibly express. Perhaps that's my devilishly handsome good looks . . . after all she is always saying I was a good catch!

Ann:

From the moment Dave and I went out together at school I knew I wanted to marry him, even though at that stage we never had that serious a relationship. I have to say all the girls fancied him. He was a very good sportsman, such a good-looking bloke and totally modest – in fact incredibly shy, and very laid-back as well. So much so that sometimes you wouldn't have even known he was in the room. He was just a really good, genuine person, so kind and generous-hearted. He was everything you wanted in a man. He probably could have had anyone and in fact he did have quite few girlfriends at school – pretty much always the girl the other guys fancied. I wasn't prone to playing the field, though. In fact, I didn't go out with any of the other guys at school.

When Dave finished with me (we had this common room at school and he just started not coming), naturally I was upset – but even more so when I found he'd ditched me for the ugliest girl you could imagine. And I'm not exaggerating. We used to call her 'fish lips'. I'd better not name her because she might read the book at some stage! Anyway, when we got back together, a year or so later, it was all set up by a guy called Dave Smith, a good friend of Dave's, who we had both been at school with. We only ever knew him as 'Bomb Head' because he had this enormous head. Cruel aren't they, teenage schoolchildren. His brother was 'Bomb Head one' and Dave was 'Bomb Head two'.

That happened because Dave Smith and I both worked at the same Liverpool department store and he was always saying to me, during lunch hours and coffee breaks, how much Dave still really fancied me. I, of course, still fancied him too.

I especially remember one story. I used to go home from work on the bus with a friend – it was about half an hour's journey – and one day, when we pulled up at her stop in Halewood, these legs came down the stairs from the top floor. You could only see the guy from the waist down and I remember my friend saying to me, "cor, look at the nuts on him!" Needless to say, it was Dave. My heart was fluttering as I got off and within a few days Bomb Head, who had been trying to get us back together again, said Dave wanted to see me again. Dave has always insisted it was a blind date for him, but I still don't believe him.

I think secretly he knew damn well it was me. We still argue about it, in fact.

Anyway, when we did meet up, at the top of a road we both knew, it was all rather embarrassing. We were walking to the bus stop to go to Woolton and Dave's mum, who I had not met at that stage, came driving past with his sister and as she tooted the horn, both of them screamed "ooOoo" out of the window because he was with a girl.

I never dreamed Dave would become a professional footballer. In my head I thought he'd be a merchant seaman – he always told me he was going to go into the navy. I had visions of being the wife of a merchant seaman and all which that entailed. In some ways I suppose the life we've had has been roughly similar, with him being away from home working intensively for long periods, although the media spotlight has been far greater, of course.

Once I'd got to know Dave and his dedication to his job, it didn't surprise me when he became a footballer that he was the model professional and would often leave his opponents standing. On a Friday night before a game, he'd be in bed by eight at the latest. That's the kind of focussed person he was – and still is. It's another of his great qualities. If he says I'm the love of his life, the feeling is certainly mutual.

Dave:
Most people I hung around with ended up marrying someone they went to school with as none of us went away to university, or met people outside our own area. Even so it was a big step for the two of us. At that point I was only on the first rung of the ladder and without Everton's help there was no way I could have afforded a house. I just wasn't earning enough money at the time. But as soon as I got married, they gave me a pay rise and we bought that first home.

Thankfully Ann always loved football and is very knowledgeable about the game and, particularly, the people in it. She attends the vast majority of matches at the clubs I manage and when I was a player, she never missed a game, home or away. She used to travel with my mum and dad all over the country to watch me. Dad always used to say to me, "get three tickets, two together, one as far away from the other two as possible." He loathed sitting with Ann and mum because they were always shouting and screaming. Dad was a bit like me, he was quiet and just wanted to watch the game.

When I became an established first teamer, Ann – ever enthusiastic – played for the Everton wives in charity matches. At least she didn't have to face me then!

PLAYING FOR
MY HEROES

AS EARLY AS 17 I was on the up and making an impression on the professional game. Wolves manager Bill McGarry wanted to sign me, but Billy Bingham wouldn't have it. He wanted to keep me at Everton and you could hardly blame Billy since at the time I was captain of the England youth team. But at this high point, when I had my entire career before me, during an overseas tournament I injured my knee ligaments. I recovered – partly as it turned out – but this was the start of an injury-plagued career.

That first injury put me out for four or five months, but it made me a stronger person as it put me in the treatment room alongside John Connolly, the Everton and Scotland winger, who was one of my heroes. I was like a sponge listening to John as he told me about his own playing career and the rehab he'd had to go through after breaking his leg. I grew up as a person during that time and, once rehabilitated myself, in 1975 went on to play in the England under-21 side and came close to earning a call up into Don Revie's full England squad.

Having always dreamed of playing for Everton, naturally my debut was an eagerly anticipated affair. I had come on as a substitute in the home game against Leicester, but only played the last 20 minutes – and that was as a winger after Gary Jones had come off in the days when you were only allowed one sub. My full debut was the one that really mattered and it also came against Leicester later that same year, but this time at their Filbert Street home. It was a freezing cold day in December 1974. I was marking Keith Weller, a tricky forward who wore tights under his shorts. Nowadays that's a common thing, of course, but back then it was unheard of. I always remember Billy Bingham saying to me, "if that player comes off that pitch and his tights aren't laddered, you will never play for me again!"

Suffice to say that Keith needed a new pair of tights after 90 minutes being marked by me.

The manager didn't tell me that I was in the team at left-back until the morning of the game because he didn't want me to be too nervous. Making your debut as a youngster is always going to be daunting and I remember being in the dressing room beforehand, looking around and thinking how surreal it was, wondering if this was actually happening. I must have done okay because, even though we lost 1-0, I stayed in the team.

In terms of my playing style, whatever position you played – and this had been the same during my brief time at Liverpool – you were told to watch the present incumbent of the shirt you wanted, since when you eventually took over you were expected to be as good or better than your predecessor. As a result, I modelled myself on John Hurst and Roger Kenyon, Everton's existing centre-halves, but I didn't have the same physical presence as them. I never set out to fight anyone in case my opponent was stronger than me. 'Be cleverer than that,' was what I told myself. That's what I tell my players now at Cardiff: be cagey if you get wound up. Neither, though, was I a flair player. I guess I was a typical bread-and-butter centre-half, someone you couldn't do without. Everton had a lot of flair players, but you also need to have your down-to-earth, no-nonsense players who will get the job done in any team. Remember the old cowboy film, *F-Troop*? Well that's what seven of us were known as, the likes of myself, Mick Lyons and Trevor Ross – those of us who regularly stuck together. It's almost impossible to get across the camaraderie we had and some of the antics we got up to. So much goes on in football that is never told. But this book is not about kiss and tell, so I won't go down that road. If I did I'd probably end up like Salmon Rushdie – going into hiding or having to leave the country because a fatwa had been declared on me by half the footballers in the England.

There are, nevertheless, some wonderful anecdotes I can tell you about, that won't do anyone any major harm. One of them my former Everton team-mate Duncan McKenzie often recalls as part of his after-dinner speech routine. It was 1976 and we were on a promotional end-of-season trip for a tournament in Egypt. We were playing the Egyptian national team and Czechoslovakia, as the country was back then, who had just won the European Championship by inflicting on the Germans in the final their only ever defeat on penalties. As we got to the stadium there must have been 1,000 people on the pitch cutting the grass . . . with scissors! If you think that's odd, wait till you hear about Gordon Lee's exchange with a group of Egyptian reporters. Now Gordon couldn't speak French and had to rely on Duncan, who had played in Belgium, to interpret for him. As our plane landed, Gordon was asked whether he was pleased to be in Africa. "Africa?" he replied in English. "We're not in Africa, we're in Egypt." Duncan, trying his best to cover up for Gordon, gave a somewhat different and more diplomatic translation. "The gaffer is very happy to be here," Duncan told the assembled local scribes.

"What do you know of Czechoslovakia team?" was another question. "Nothing, never seen 'em," replied Gordon. This was translated by Duncan as "he thinks they're a very good side, it'll be a good test for us."

By the time Duncan had finished Gordon was being hailed as a majestic diplomat by the press and all the lads were absolutely wetting themselves.

Gordon was something else, I tell you. On another occasion, he was driving all the way up the motorway to Newcastle to watch a game and Steve Burtenshaw, his assistant, gently reminded him that he was driving in slippers. Gordon had forgotten to put his shoes on and so he watched the game in full suit and slippers. That was Gordon all over.

Duncan McKenzie's French wasn't the only thing that marked him out from everyone else. Not only was he a brilliant footballer, but a fantastic man – and still is. He was never afraid of sending himself up. I remember when he signed for Everton he put his arm around then manager Billy Bingham and said he didn't know why Billy had signed him because every other manager who had done so left within three months. Billy laughed.

And guess what, the same thing happened to Billy! It had nothing to do with Duncan, just a coincidence as a poor run of form cost the gaffer his job.

I got to know Duncan quite well because I used to room with him. He used to bore me rigid by playing football quiz games like naming a full England side beginning with A. Then we'd go through the same thing with B and on through the whole flaming alphabet. Then he'd start on countries beginning with A etc. I used to fall asleep with my eyes open. But he was a lovely guy for whom I have enormous respect.

Duncan typified the maverick player of the era; he and others like Rodney Marsh and Alan Hudson. Duncan had unbelievable ability, but like so many flair players he could drive you crazy. You could be under the cosh and when you gave him the ball he'd try to do something special and lose it, putting you back under pressure. But his ability was frightening at times. We accepted the occasional errors, knowing he would do more good things than bad.

EVERY PLAYER HAS notable highlights in his career and the 1977 League Cup final has to be one of mine, though in the build-up to the game I thought my chance of playing at Wembley had gone. Everton had signed Bruce Rioch, the Scotland captain, but he couldn't play in the final – which we'd reached after beating Cambridge, Stockport, Coventry, Manchester United, with a fabulous 3-0 victory at Old Trafford, and Bolton over two legs in the semi-final – because he was cup-tied, having played for Derby earlier in the tournament. The day before the final we were training and a ball came towards me in the air. As I concentrated on the dropping ball, Bruce ran from about ten yards away on my blind side and took me out completely. I had stud marks all down my chin and was completely dazed just 24 hours before the biggest game of my life. I looked at Bruce and managed to move my jaw enough to ask, "what the f*** are you doing?" I'll always remember his reply. "You'll do for me, son, you don't pull out of tackles." Or so he thought. I hadn't seen him coming. Had I done so, of course, I would have jumped a mile. There was no way I was going to be injured before the cup final.

With some intensive treatment I recovered in time only for a drab game at Wembley against Aston Villa to be drawn 0-0. Well 'drab' is how the media described it. I remember it being a hard, physical game, but we nearly won it in the last minute. I remember the whole day, even down to clearing up the spurs that had been left behind on the pitch by the band that had been playing before kick-off. In the evening we went for the routine post-cup final celebratory meal because everyone had thought the game would be settled on the day. For me, as an Evertonian, to play in a cup final at Wembley stadium was the stuff of dreams.

The first replay at Hillsborough was only marginally better, but at least Bob Latchford managed a last-minute equaliser, after Roger Kenyon had scored an own goal to give Villa the lead, which took us to Old Trafford .

In the second replay it was Villa who scored late on to lift the cup 3-2. That followed one of the most remarkable cup final goals of all time when Villa centre-half Chris Nicholl picked the ball up right on the touchline, cut inside and smacked a shot with his left foot from all of 40 yards past our keeper David Lawson. It was a fantastic shot and, coupled with Brian Little's two goals, gave Villa the trophy.

I didn't play in either replay because I was injured yet again and didn't recover. But it wasn't only reaching the League Cup final that gave me such a thrill that season. Swindon at home in the FA Cup fourth round really sticks in my mind since that was when I scored my first goal for the club – and what an important goal it was. As it happens, it was also Gordon Lee's first game as manager after taking over from Billy, so scoring certainly didn't do me any harm. It was a freezing night and I remember Gordon coming to the ground without a coat and having to borrow Martin Dobson's sheepskin. We should have known then he was a bit different. Anyway, we were going out of the tournament after Swindon scored first, but three minutes later we equalised. Then, late on, yours truly struck the winner. It was a fantastic feeling. I just remember picking the ball up on the halfway line and looking to pass. A gap opened up in front of me and I went through it and then I struck my shot from about 30 yards out. It took a deflection and looped up and over the goalkeeper. It seemed to take an eternity. For any player to score for his home club is unbelievable, but to do it on that night with so much at stake made it feel that much better. It was especially sweet for me that it happened at the Gwladys Street end as that was the end where I had stood as a kid.

Everton had an attitude when they played teams in a lower division of 'get in, be calculated, and get out.' That happened on our way to Wembley in several rounds before the semi-final against Bolton. You would never see it now, but in those days everyone had a little swig of whisky before they ran out on the pitch. Some would even consume as much as half a bottle. I'm not a shorts drinker so I never touched the stuff, but there was always a bottle of whisky on the table. Cigarettes, though, were a different matter which is why I'll never forget, after we won the semi against Bolton through Bob Latchford's goal, everyone having a smoke in the bath. We had one of those big communal baths and I just shook my head at the sight of trained athletes smoking. Not that I didn't know about various players' smoking habits. We used to joke, in fact, that Duncan McKenzie had a cigarette machine in the toilet. At half-time, he and Mick Bernard often used to disappear for a puff.

As an Everton player, Merseyside derbies were, of course, extra special and I played in five of them. The first, in 1976, was nerve-wracking because of the fact I was up against players like Kevin Keegan, John Toshack, Phil Thompson and a certain Tommy Smith. I'd played in all kinds of games, but nothing matched this – 50,000 people at Anfield. My legs felt like jelly even 90 minutes before the game. Just before we went out there was a bang on our dressing room door and as we opened it, loads of toilet rolls were thrown at us. In other words, if you're not sh****** yourselves now, you soon will be.

The atmosphere was frightening, but one thing helped relax me. When we were warming up there was a pigeon on the pitch that had damaged its wing. It was picked up by Terry Darracott, our right-back. When they saw him snare the injured bird, the Liverpool coaching staff shouted to their winger Steve Heighway, "Steve, change wings and play against that lad Jones. This full-back can catch pigeons!" That was typical of the sense of humour between the teams at that time. All my mates were there, everyone I knew in fact, all rooting for red or blue. We lost the game 1-0 in the last few minutes when David Fairclough – Liverpool's super-sub – came on and scored. Somewhere there is a picture of me lying on the pitch crying. I was only 19 and didn't take defeat well, but I'd played really well and came out of the game with a lot of credit.

It was not a nice experience losing at Anfield, though, and neither was being beaten by Liverpool in the FA Cup semi-final, also in 1977. Like the League Cup final against Villa, that tie went to a replay, but not before experienced midfielder Bryan Hamilton looked to have won the first game for us, only for the referee to disallow the goal for handball. In the replay we got battered 3-0 and once again I was devastated to lose out on such a big stage.

Speaking of Everton-Liverpool games, one that sticks firmly in my memory came a year or so earlier when I had to face Tommy Smith in a reserve team derby at Anfield while the seniors were playing at Goodison. In those days, if you couldn't get into the main game as a fan, you used to go and watch the reserve derby which could attract as many as 15,000. In this game a 50-50 ball was played between me and Tommy and, being younger than the Liverpool warhorse, as I chased it, it was becoming more like 60-40 in my favour, then 70-30. Suddenly I realised who it was coming in to tackle me and I looked up and knew instantly that Tommy was going to do me. At that point we both left the ball completely and lunged at each other. The problem was I slipped right up the inside of his leg. Not the cleverest thing to do to the man with the most fearsome reputation in the game. As we picked ourselves up off the floor, Tommy turned round to me and these were his exact words: "Son, I'm going to knock nine different coloured bags of shite out of you." For some reason, I replied: "Shut it, beans-on-toast face." It was the first thing that came into my head. Well, he did have all those pock-marks on his face, didn't he?

After the game, as we got down the tunnel, I wasn't going to back down, even though the lads kept warning me Tommy was following me, fuming. As he approached me I thought he was going to hit me for doing him, but instead Tommy put his arm round me and said, "Well done, son."

What a side Everton had in those days. The School of Science, they used to call it, and that's what it felt like. Even Bill Shankly thought so. Don't believe me? Shankly's house backed on to our training ground and he used to come and watch us kids, even though we were all only 17 and 18. In fact he tried to persuade me to sign for Liverpool – even though the club had dropped me a couple of years earlier. The evening of the day I signed pro forms for Everton, Shankly tried to make me change my mind. My mentors at Everton were John Hurst, Roger Kenyon and Mick Lyons and Shankly knew I modelled myself on the three of them. Hurst was pure class and never got flustered, Kenyon was more aggressive and Lyons, who is now living in Australia, was blue all the way through. Shankly told me he wanted me to become his new Tommy Smith. Talk about tapping up, *that's* tapping up. Shankly even came to my house, but I'd already put pen to paper for Everton and I was never going to shift. After all I'd realised my dream. For me Everton's a special club. My club. Even now, when I go back to watch games, I am treated like a king, the local boy come good. Blue was always in my heart, not red.

The feeling is totally mutual: the list of players I had the privilege of playing with at Goodison reads like a who's who. Martin Dobson was the Trevor Brooking of the time – a midfield goalscorer and a real gentleman, just like the former TV character 'Hadley', after whom he was nicknamed. Martin was Mr. Cool and casual.

Mick Lyons became a really good friend of mine, not least because he and Roger Kenyon took me under their wing and became the senior players I aspired to emulate. Mick was a diehard blue who would run through brick walls and never give up on anything. Before he went out to play, if he didn't head-butt the ceiling he didn't think he'd have a good game. There weren't actually many ceilings he didn't manage to butt! He never ever swore, even though we played some unbelievable tricks on him, mostly perpetrated by a cheeky-chappy midfielder named Andy King. Mick was a devout Catholic and we'd often hide his rosary beads, but two somewhat more unusual instances stand out, though I'm not sure Mick would appreciate me reciting them. In the first, how shall I put it politely, we 'played around' with a toothbrush and put it back in Mick's tray. When he got up in the morning and cleaned his teeth, well I daren't tell you where it had been.

That pales into insignificance, though, compared to a time when Mick was ill. He'd been banished to his room so as not to make contact with any of the other players in case he passed this bug on. We knew he'd ordered room service and when it arrived it was on a silver platter. We took the food off and someone – I won't say who – crapped on the plate, then put the dome back on. Ann refuses to believe that I played any part in it. What I can put down on record is that it was the only time that Mick came even close to swearing. I know it sounds disgusting, but that was the kind of stuff that went on, it was all part of the camaraderie. When you can play jokes on each other and it's accepted without any animosity or bad feeling, that's when you know you have a strong group and we had that in spades at Everton. That's why I'm such a strong believer, as a manager, that if you get a group of people who can have a go at one another – and be quite ruthless if necessary – yet still smile and have a laugh and not bear any grudges, it counts for so much.

We used to fall out regularly at Everton both on the pitch and in training, but it never ever spilled over. I always tell my players that if someone is not doing his job, you tell him – but, crucially, in a way that is not disrespectful. I always say that if they are not enjoying training to say so, to keep everything open and tell me, so that we can try and make it better. After all, none of us are mind readers. If they feel something is not right, it's important for them to express it and for me as manager to find out why.

Going back to the Everton players in my day, goals win games and Bob Latchford was the main man in that respect. He came to Everton from Birmingham City in part-exchange for one of my idols, Howard Kendall. For me growing up Everton *was* Ball, Harvey and Kendall, who I had played with in the reserves in the early part of my career. They had to have been one of the best midfield trios ever. They complemented each other so well. Colin in fact was known as the 'white Pelé'.

Latch didn't disappoint. He was quiet but, as they say, did his talking on the pitch. Roger Kenyon was quite different. I remember him having a car crash and coming in to training a couple of days later with his face all scarred. All of a sudden, as we were running round the pitch, blood started spurting from Roger's neck. There was still, incredibly, a piece of glass lodged in one of his veins. But he was such a hard guy it didn't bother him. Roger was probably one of the hardest I have ever come across in my life. Let me give you another example. One of my first games for Everton was against Coventry, who had a centre-forward named Ernie Hunt. Ernie was, quite frankly, a horrible player to be up against, a nasty piece of work. In the tunnel before the game I lined up alongside him and Ernie turned to me and asked if it was my debut. Before I could say it wasn't, he spat at me, presumably to unsettle me. I then heard this shout from the back. It was Roger. "That's the last thing you'll do today, Ernie," he stated. And it was. After about 15 seconds on the pitch, Roger went through this fella like no-one's business and looked at me as if to say, 'that's how you repay someone for the kind of thing he did.'

When you were a young player in those days, one of the unwritten rules was that you looked after the senior players when they'd had a few beers. I always remember being in a hotel room with Mick Bernard and Roger as they were on the gin and tonic. They kept the ice in the sink and it was my job to get it for them. But when I got tired of fetching it, they thought it would be a good idea to pull the sink off the wall to get the ice nearer the bed. Result? I was up half the night with my fingers stuck in the holes in the wall trying to stop water pouring out of where the pipes should have been!

There's another story I must tell you concerning striker Imre Varadi, or at least my impersonation of him. We were playing the 1977 League Cup final and Joe Mercer, the legendary old Everton and England half-back, who was a club guest, was coming down in the hotel lift with me. For some unknown reason he thought I was Imre. Without wanting to be in any way disrespectful since Joe was getting on a bit and got us mixed up, I proceeded to talk to him as if I was indeed Imre. I simply didn't have the heart to tell Joe who I really was. I did play with Imre actually, but not on many occasions. He was brought up in a really hard part of the Sheffield area and had to sleep in the dugout at one point during his apprenticeship at Sheffield United when he didn't have a home. Considering the start in life Imre had, to go on and have the great career he did with clubs like Everton, Manchester City, Newcastle United and both Sheffield sides, amongst others, he did fantastically well.

I can honestly say there were not many players at Everton I didn't get along with. Most of them were characters. Even though he played after I did, John Bailey was known as the 'entertainments officer'. I remember playing with John in a legends game at Wembley before Everton defeated Manchester United in the 1995 FA Cup final. I don't think John even knew he was there, he'd enjoyed himself so much the night before. After we had won the match we couldn't get another old Everton legend, Dave Hickson, off the pitch because he kept running round with the trophy, even though they were getting ready to bring on the two teams and the band for the showpiece event!

Speaking of full-backs, Mike 'Peji' Pejic used to be known as 'Peji the farmer'. He bought Kevin Keegan's farm in north Wales when Kevin moved to Hamburg and used to turn up for training in a battered old Landrover. One day he arrived with a lamb in the back! I had a lot of time for Peji. He had the flattest nose in football and one summer had it rebuilt. Problem was, in his very first game back, someone smashed it. You win some, you lose some.

Almost every one of the characters I played with at that time with had a personality of their own. Terry Darracott was the comedian of the group. He was a fantastic guy as well and he and his wife adopted twins. The best way to describe him was that if you wanted to be adopted by somebody, Terry would be the ideal person. We went away one year on a pre-season tour – one of my first with the first team – and the hotel we were staying in had a couple of massive concrete balls on the landing, I guess they were there just for show. We decided to play our own version of pinball and rolled one of them down the stairs. Terry tried to save it, crushing his hand in the process. He was always up to something. On another occasion, while in Puerto Banus in Spain, Terry dismantled the hotel piano just for a laugh.

Last but not least, there was goalkeeper George Wood and in writing this book I pause before deciding how to describe George. Why? For the simple reason that, give him a drink and he was a man possessed. Stay out the way of George Wood on the booze! One year over the Christmas period, George was stopped in his car and, when he opened his door to get out and chat to the policeman, proceeded to fall out onto the verge. It was the day before we were playing Manchester United and I remember the management going to pick him from the cells to take him to the game. You were only allowed one substitute then – and no replacement keeper, so there was no back up for George. The coaches were pumping coffee into him right up to the game, but luckily for him he never touched the ball. We won 3-0. It was the first time Everton had ever played five centre-backs, four across the defence and one as a holding midfielder – all to protect Woody!

Away from the pitch there was, of course, a thriving social scene on Merseyside. I, like many others, had long hair, but I didn't really get caught up in what was going on. People often talk about the so-called Liverpool mafia and there was this particular gentleman who used to come to Everton – I'd better not name him. Every club, though, had someone who was known in the gangster world, but I avoided being part of anything like that. I was brought up in the right way and I wasn't tempted by any of it. Often someone would say to you that they were going out drinking, but I always felt able to say no, even though it would have been easy to get caught up in the nightclub scene. I always believe players should be treated as men. I don't believe in bans and curfews particularly. I allow my players at Cardiff to drink in moderation. They are adults after all. But – and it's a major but – if they don't perform come game time, they know what the consequences are.

MOVING ON

LIVERPOOL MAY HAVE been winning things more regularly than us on the other side of Stanley Park, but we didn't exactly live in their shadow. Gordon Lee probably won't like me saying it, but as a manager now looking back at that time, I can say with all honesty that Everton weren't far off matching Liverpool. The problem was he couldn't pull all the gifted players together to make a team to truly challenge for honours. Players I haven't mentioned – like Colin Todd, Andy King and Dave Thomas – were all worth their salt and more. We finished third in 1977/78 and fourth the following season, playing a stylish type of game, but, as I say, Gordon just couldn't hold it all together. That's probably why we didn't kick on during that period.

I'm as pleased as anyone that Everton went on to be so successful under Howard Kendall in the mid-1980s, but at the same time it's my biggest regret that I didn't stay, even for just one more season, and become part of Howard's team. He actually told me later that he'd have picked me. Instead a managerial decision made by Gordon Lee as his team spiralled into a run of games without winning to struggle along near the bottom of the table resulted in my biggest regret in football.

Everton was the only club I ever wanted to play for and I'd now been established in the team for several years and everything seemed to be going swimmingly until I received a phone call out of the blue from Gordon Lee to tell me that Coventry had come in for me and he thought

I should leave and that it would be good career move. I was at the height of *my* career at *my* club and Lee's remarks hit me like a bombshell: let's face it, Everton were a much bigger club than Coventry. But I wanted to play at centre-half and at the time Everton had an abundance of them. Gordon wanted me to stick to full-back and I thought that was curtailing my potential international career, so I signed for Coventry manager Gordon Milne for £275,000.

What choice did I have? Lee made it clear that if I stayed I would only ever be used as a full-back. Just before I put pen to paper, Bobby Robson contacted Everton to say he wanted me at Ipswich to play alongside Kevin Beattie. It was tempting as Ipswich were a very good side with the likes of Alan Brazil, Arnold Muhren and John Wark playing some wonderful football, but I had given my word to Coventry. Ipswich just came in too late. Okay, they had Bobby Robson in charge and we now know what he went on to achieve, but I always try to turn a negative into a positive. If I'd gone and signed for Ipswich I might not be on the road I'm on now. Besides, Gordon Milne sold me the club and Coventry had some darned good players, not least Ian Wallace, Mick Ferguson, Stevie Hunt and Tommy Hutchinson. They'd finished in 10th position in 1978/79 and all the talk from Gordon, which I have to say convinced me to sign, was of pushing on towards European qualification.

It was a real wrench to leave my own environment, but we only had our eldest child at that point; Lea, our son. Our first daughter Danielle was born while we were at Coventry and while I'm on the subject, Chloe was born while I was at Preston and I was playing in non-league when our youngest, Georgia, came along.

The problems began as soon as I arrived when the club started cashing in all their best talent. Wallace was sold to Nottingham Forest for a huge £1.25m fee, Hutchison went to Manchester City via a loan spell at Seattle Sounders and Ferguson ironically joined Everton. Gordon Milne had basically got me there under false pretences. He had promised the earth, but didn't deliver. I'd signed to play centre-half alongside Gary Collier, an England under-21 colleague and another young up-and-coming defender whom they signed at the same time for £325,000 from Bristol City. Gary only played one game. And I felt I was permanently messed about. It only took six months for me to feel that I didn't want to be at the club any more. In the event I stayed another two years. Nice club, nice people, but sometimes when you're not enjoying yourself it's a recipe for niggling injuries and that's what happened to me.

The huge positive for me from that otherwise grim time was that Coventry is where I met my best mate in football, goalkeeper Les Sealey. Les was totally off the wall and egged me on to get up to all sorts. We used to room together and I remember one time, when we went to Greece, we decided to play a trick on the other players. We filled a load of balloons up with water, stripped naked and ran down the corridor of the hotel knocking on doors and, when they opened, pelting the players. The problem was the police were called by the hotel staff and we turned one particular corner, totally starkers, to be confronted by members of the Greek constabulary and hotel security. 'Boll****,' all those present undoubtedly thought. Not surprisingly, the officers took a firm grip on the situation and we were taken back to our rooms with a stern warning ringing in our ears.

Les and I became bosom buddies and he was one of the major reasons I stayed at Highfield Road, although with the continuing injury problems I suffered I couldn't really see anyone else wanting to sign me. Despite my personal struggles, there were plenty of other stories to make you laugh. Jimmy Hill was the chairman at the time and used to take us to his house at the end of every season to negotiate our contracts. One year we went into his dining room, where Jimmy had this table made out of a door which was probably thousands of years old and worth a fortune and Les suddenly piped up: "friggin 'eck (that was his favourite expression), look lads, we're gonna be eating off a door." Les, being Les, didn't quite see the historic or aesthetic value the same way Jimmy did.

The only problem with Les was that he had the shortest of fuses. If you had a stick of dynamite, best not to give it to Les because if he didn't like you, you'd had it. Ron Wylie and Gordon Milne had this training regime which involved what we used to call the embankment. Ron would point in one direction or the other and you had to run the way he pointed, but if you ended up being sent 'over the hill', that meant you weren't in the first team. We used to wind Les up by saying he was going 'over the hill', so much so that he was ready to explode. Once, as assistant-manager Ron Wylie was standing and pointing to who he wanted to run where, Les ran straight up to him, stuck one on Ron, then ran over the hill. That was Les.

I remember one particular flashpoint between us when I gave a backpass to him in a game. The ball ended up in the net and Les chased me the length of the pitch to throw a punch at me because he'd missed it and given the goal away. And he was my best mate! He was the Arthur Daley of his time, but Ann and I loved him and his wife, Elaine.

We seemed blessed with our fair share of nutters at Coventry. There was the strange case of Dave Bradshaw, an ex-Blackburn winger who had been playing in America. One of the deals Jimmy Hill had done was to bring Dave back into this country by buying out his contract, even though Dave didn't actually want to return. He didn't play many games and as a protest of being brought back to England against his will went to the extreme one night of knocking the headlights out of every club car with a hammer in order to get sacked. He eventually did leave, although I think Jimmy Hill kept him on as long as he could just for a bit of revenge.

Les Sealey went on to star for Luton Town and win the FA Cup and two League Cups with Manchester United, always in his own inimitable, bubbly style as he played on into his 40th year. It was such a shock when Les died in August 2001. I was managing Wolves at the time and I was travelling back from a game at Coventry, strangely enough, when I got a call telling me Les had died. He had felt pains in his chest and just dropped dead. He had never had a day's illness in his life and was the West Ham goalkeeping coach at the time. He was just 43 years old. It is days like that which make you thankful for everything you've got. Even though by then I'd been through the hideous experience of the court case and was still dealing with the fallout, I thanked my lucky stars that night and offered a little prayer for Les.

After about 18 months at Coventry I got injured again, picking up serious cruciate ligament damage. While I was recovering from injury, a team from Hong Kong named after sponsors Seiko, the watch company, came over to train for a week. It was nearing the end of our season and I played against them to test my fitness. It was clear I needed games and one way of getting them was to go over to Hong Kong to play for them, which I did for three months. It was a question of 'have boots, will travel', but when I got back I realised I wasn't completely cured. Nevertheless, Jim Smith tried to sign me at Oxford who were flying at the time on their way up the leagues to the big time.

I sat up all night chatting with Jim when, out of the blue, there was the first in a series of hilarious telephone exchanges with Hong Kong. At around 2am, I got a phone call from the boss of Bulova, the other main watch company there (they were both, incidentally, run by the Wong brothers – one C.P Wong, the other K.P. Wong). Bulova were managed by Ron Wylie who, in his previous job, had been Gordon Milne's number two at Coventry. So much in football is about those contacts and relationships.

"Would you fancy going back to Hong Kong and playing for me?" Ron asked. I told Ann it would be good money as well as an opportunity to test my fitness. But, no sooner had I put the phone down on Ron than Seiko rang and told me I couldn't possibly play for their rivals. In fact they would pay me even more – tax free, of course! Nuff said. I agreed and the next thing I knew I was playing for a representative side against Brazil, with Bobby Moore as our manager. It was a fabulous experience. Jairzinho and Socrates were in the Brazil team and we managed to draw 1-1. What a lovely man Bobby was – a real gentleman, who set a wonderful example, always having time to speak to people. But life wasn't to everyone's taste out there. A lot of players who came across couldn't cope with the weather, food, or times of training. I, on the other hand, bought into it and after a couple of weeks was joined by Ann and the two kids after she'd sold our house. We had a wonderful time out in the Far East, but after a year or so, my knee, lacking the ligament completely now, couldn't take any more.

In fact, the medical people warned me that if I didn't leave, I'd end up in a wheelchair. I went to see the main man, the aforementioned Mr C.P. Wong, and said I couldn't stay, even though I was signed on for another season. I wish I could have fulfilled my contract; I was treated like a king, as a god – and I embraced the Chinese players who were playing with me. I did the job properly and we had a proud record. In my 18 months there, when I played I never lost a game. All the teams were multi-national, though we didn't have any other English players in ours. The standard was lower than what I was used to, but I never slackened just because I was getting good money. We were streets ahead of any other side and, on top of that, there were some seriously hilarious moments. If it was 0-0 at half-time, the chairman used to come in to the dressing room and offer us more bonus money to go on and win the game. The Chinese players soon got the hang of it. "Keep score down till half-time," they'd say, "then boss panic and more money." Capitalism ruled, even back in 1981!

It was a wrench to leave, but when I did, Mr Wong handed me an envelope as a gift. It wasn't protocol to open it in front of the boss, but when I did I found they had paid my wages up for the whole of the following year as a thank you for doing so well for them.

The money was gratefully received, even though it was a big surprise, because my playing career was over – or so I thought. When we returned to the UK, I had no idea what to do. I thought maybe I'd buy a pub – as footballers did then – or maybe buy a truck to do long-distance haulage because I loved driving.

First off we had to get back into the UK without having half of the bonus ripped off me by the taxman. We actually touched down in the country from Hong Kong a little too soon in terms of how much tax we would have to pay, so Ann and I quietly flew straight out to Turkey for a few weeks' R&R.

As I was considering what to do whilst enjoying myself at the eastern end of the Med, I got a phone call from Gordon Lee who had sold me from Everton to Coventry. He was now in charge at Preston and asked me whether I'd go and help him out for a few games because he only had one fully fit centre-half. He asked me if I was fit and I said I was, but that my knee could go any day. It didn't, thankfully, and I ended up playing for two seasons in the same team as my brother, Mark, who was Preston's full-back. Mark won't like me for saying this but he had the attitude which was 'tomorrow will do' – similar to my son. I feel that with a bit more dedication and commitment both would have gone a long way within the professional game. I'd have done anything to be a footballer – and did – whereas my brother was not dedicated enough to make the best of his talent in the professional game in truth, although he went on to become a top player in the non-league game. Unfortunately my son Lea had to end his professional career prematurely at Stockport due to a bone that he broke in his back during training.

PLAYING HAD TO come to an end for me at some point. My knee was always liable to buckle under the strain and eventually it did. We were playing Lincoln City right near the end of the 1984/85 season and as a ball came out of the air and I went to kick it, my knee rotated, but the lower half of my leg didn't and the shooting pain was absolute agony. I knew then it was time to pack it in. It wasn't so much the playing, but all the pounding in training. After all the operations there were no ligaments inside either knee any more. They'd snapped and the surgical techniques and treatments which are available now had not been developed then.

I was devastated when it all ended. Football was everything I'd known and I was packing it up in my late-20s. To be honest I felt cheated. I'd damaged my right knee first as a 17-year-old playing for England youth, but I sort of got over it after being operated on and being helped in my recuperation by John Connolly. It was the left one that really gave me problems, starting at Coventry. If I could have got hold of the lad who did it I'd have killed him because it was the beginning of the end and took away any chance I had of a full international career. It happened in a reserve game early in my time at Highfield Road. I sidestepped the guy – I have never revealed his name and never will, I simply don't see the point. He didn't mean to end my career – and as I did so, he came in from the blind side and took my knee away, snapping the ligament. The physio came on and told me I was okay, so I continued, but when, moments later, I jumped for a corner, the bottom of my leg stayed where it was. I was on a downward slope from then.

Looking back at the standard of diagnosis and treatment I received back then I do feel it was extremely poor. At one stage they told me they weren't even sure I had any ligaments to start with – but I had heard the snap. The way I was treated then affected me deeply and is the major reason why I'm so big on preventative work when we are looking after our players at Cardiff. Injuries are the same now as then. Yes modern medical care is far more advanced and allows players to get back a lot quicker. But I firmly believe that wasn't the reason for my sustained problem. It seemed that, right from the very start, they cocked up the diagnosis, leading me to cause more and more damage to my knees until it finished me.

Yet you know something? You have to be a bit philosophical about these things. What I mean by that is that if the injury hadn't happened to me, I wouldn't be where I am now in terms of the managerial path I took. I guess I'll never know what the other path might have been.

The reality of finishing playing professionally didn't take long to kick in. I joined non-league Southport as assistant player-manager to Bryan Griffiths, another ex-Evertonian, although in his case from the late-1950s. I loved it, really got into coaching and knew straight away where I wanted to go with my career. But as it was non-league we got nothing more than expenses payments. I had bills to pay and three hungry mouths to feed, so I needed a job and my savings weren't going to last for ever. I went for various interviews including being a salesman for a paint company owned by the Southport chairman, but that wasn't for me. No chance. Bryan had given me my first taste of wanting to be a manager in that 1986/87 season and, after something of a fallout with the Southport owner, we then took up identical roles at Mossley in 1988. I was firmly on my path. I was going to be a football manager. That's all I had in my mind as I attended a number of interviews for jobs which would pay the bills while I gained the badges, experience and credibility to enable myself to apply for full-time Football League positions.

Little did I know, when I applied for a job as a care worker at the Clarence House school in the Freshfield area of Formby, how it would end up shaping the rest of my life.

GISSA JOB

IT WAS ANN who first saw the advert in our local paper saying Clarence House, a special school for children with behavioural problems in Merseyside, were recruiting. It was the kind of place kids went when mainstream schools couldn't cope with them any more. I would never have dreamed of going for the job, partly, I suppose, because my tolerance levels of people misbehaving are not the highest – and these were youngsters who had been into drugs, thieving, you name it. Some of them would spit in your face, try to fight you, while others were simply from broken homes. Before I even begin to discuss working there, let me say that two of the people I was recruited with, Dina Nixon and Joanne O'Neil, are still among my closest friends – as is Dina's husband John. They always will be because of the way they solidly backed me during the dark days of my child abuse case.

My Clarence House interview was relatively straightforward, not least because, by pure coincidence, the person who interviewed me just happened to have been the Liverpool county schoolboys manager when I was at school about 18 years earlier. I didn't even recognise him. I had to take a small exam, but because of my background in football, they were keen on employing me to work with behavioural problem boys. Getting them in the gym and playing football were just the type of therapeutic measures they felt would help get through to these kids.

You may think I must have been mad going for this kind of thing – it was seven days a week – but I saw it simply as just a job to get me the next step towards where I wanted to go. I was desperate to get back into football as my sole source of income and undoubtedly the Clarence House experience helped me. All through my time there, it must have been about three years in all, I was coaching part-time either at South-port, Mossley or Morecambe, where Bryan and I moved on to in 1989, all non-league clubs. The wages from the job at Clarence House just about covered the bills and our savings dwindled over this period until I got myself a full-time coaching role at Stockport County in 1990.

Because I was on a rota at the school which required I be on duty on Tuesday and Thursday nights (the very time I was supposed to be taking training at Southport) Dina used to help me, even though she hated football with a passion. She would help me pile the kids in the bus; I'd take them to training and she would sit in the stands with them, then we'd pile them back in the bus, take them back to Clarence House and give them supper. Without her, I could never have done both tasks. Without that I may not have begun to climb the rungs of football coaching into management. The kids loved it. It was a social experience for them and also gave them some structure and a little bit of purpose in their life.

I began working in what they called the 38-week unit at Clarence House, but after about eight months got transferred to the 52-week unit. This was exactly what it said on the tin – kids placed there 52 weeks of the year. We had such a variety of children, some of them from seem-ingly good homes. One was even a Magistrate's child. But unfortunately a lot of them were unruly and couldn't be controlled at home, so they were placed in care either by the courts or the local authorities. I'd start work around 7.30 in the morning, making sure the kids got up, washed, were fed and ready on time to go to school which was on the same site about 50 yards away. While they were at school, I'd basically help map out their future, writing reports and helping the rest of the staff who were incredibly dedicated people. Their interest was solely for the good of the kids. It was quite strange because a lot of the people I worked with were more institutionalised than the kids themselves. It was their way of life and had been, in many cases, for years, whereas I just saw it as a means to pay my bills.

Around 18 months after I started at Clarence House, Ann joined too. We had three kids and needed the money, even though, with her working nights, it was hardly the ideal scenario for a young marriage to thrive in. It was hard, really hard, because we'd gone from a magnificent lifestyle in Hong Kong to another, so very different. Although girls were also admitted to Clarence House, I worked mainly with the boys. Because of my background in football, it was easy to break down barriers, but in truth I was never really cut out for the work. Later, when the accusations against me were flying around, I just couldn't get it across to the police that I had only been there to pay my bills. There wasn't nearly as much money around football, remember, as there is now – especially not in non-league. I had always grafted to earn a living and this had been my beginnings, which by the time of the investigation had led me, eventually, to the Premier League.

I have to admit there were times when I wondered whether I'd ever get back into full-time football. There weren't many jobs coming up. In football, it's often about who you are. Because I'd been out of it for a few years, people had begun to forget who I was. Catch 22. I had a good reputation in non-league, but not at a higher level, so, of course, I asked questions of myself. I wasn't a self-publicist and perhaps didn't put myself in the shop window enough by networking, being satisfied that my non-league management experience would eventually pay off.

You can imagine my joy, then, when I went for my first Football League job, after answering an advert for the position of youth team coach at Walsall, and got it. John Barnwell was the manager and offered me the job there and then. He walked me out to my car and on the drive home I couldn't have been happier: I was back in full-time football as I had always craved. But as I got close to home, John called me to say he'd spoken to his chairman and they had decided to give the job to the incumbent goalkeeping coach instead. Within two hours I had gone from being ecstatic to gutted. I couldn't believe it, not least because it meant spending even more time at Clarence House, which was fine in terms of carrying on earning, but not in terms of career progression.

To be honest, during a career in football you have to take the rough with the smooth, so I put that disappointment behind me quickly and, luckily, not so long afterwards, saw an advert in the paper asking for applications for the job of youth team coach at Stockport County. I duly applied, didn't hear anything for ages, then got a phone call from John Higgins, who'd played centre-half for Bolton Wanderers in the 1950s and early 1960s. He in fact played in Bolton's 2-0 win over Manchester United in the 1958 FA Cup final and his motto was 'If the ball goes past, the man doesn't.' Anyway, John was on the board at Stockport and knew me because I had played with his son Mark at Everton where we had become good friends. Stockport were in the old Fourth Division at the time and John suggested I went down to meet manager Danny Bergara. I can honestly say it was the strangest interview I've ever had in my life. Danny was Uruguayan and like all South Americans was obsessed by football. All he talked about was eating and sleeping the game and he hardly asked me anything at all. It was a case of 'I know who you are, I know your career'. Afterwards, John Higgins called me to ask how it went. "I don't really know," I replied – because I didn't. "Well you've got the job," he said. "Danny should have told you."

I soon learned that I was actually going to be given the job even before the interview took place. It was just a procedure they had to go through. I was now chuffed to bits once again, just a couple of weeks after the setback at Walsall. I was back in the Football League and on my way. I called Ann to let her know and, of course, she was delighted too. There was one somewhat important downside, however: no money. Well when I say no money, I actually mean crap money – this was the Fourth Division. But I wanted to get back into the game full-time so much that I was prepared to make a sacrifice somewhere along the line. When I got home we had a big party to celebrate.

Next day I got into work at Clarence House and told them I was leaving. They thanked me for everything I'd done at the school, though in truth the Head of Care – there were two headmasters, one Head of

Care, the other Head of School – was a bit angry because he'd put me through a lot of courses, fast-tracking me through to being a qualified care worker. He understood my reasons, though, and we parted on good terms.

Despite the fact I gave my all every moment of every day I was at Clarence House, I can't honestly say I was disappointed to leave. Much as I had enjoyed what was exhausting if rewarding work – there were kids there who had knives hidden away, there were arsonists, there were thugs – you spent much of the time sorting out who'd been fighting who, who got stabbed, that sort of thing, rather than teaching the kids anything. Luckily it didn't faze me and I had met some really good people there, and that includes some of the kids. They weren't all bad, far from it. While I was there, a young boy died and his parents wrote me a letter thanking me for looking after him. Years later, during the court case, I received letters from other parents of kids I had worked with at Clarence House telling me what a disgrace the accusations were. That meant an awful lot to me as, despite the fact I was only there as a job rather than the vocation, as it is for so many of Britain's wonderful, underrated and undervalued workers in such institutions.

Perhaps that's why I found being accused of such disgusting and degrading things by some of the kids I'd cared for in my time there so galling. I'll give you one example which still grates. One Christmas Day, Dina was on duty at Clarence House and there was one kid left on his own as everyone else had some relative or other to visit for the big day. Being the sort of person she is, rather than him having a depressing time, Dina decided to take the boy, whose name I cannot divulge for legal reasons, back to her house to have Christmas lunch with her family. He was showered with kindness, given presents and spent the whole day there. Years later this same person turned out to be one of my accusers. You have to ask yourself how and why his head was turned. It could easily have been my house he'd been invited to for Christmas and yet I'm sure he still would have accused me.

I guess this was why the staff at Clarence House had a saying about the kids: that kindness was looked upon by them as a weakness. There were no moral values with a small minority of them. That's one of the reasons why, even with my ability not to get over-emotional, Clarence House had been a difficult, demanding and trying job to go to every day. Non-league football ended up being my sanity, but what it also importantly taught me was to appreciate how tough it was for non-league players and coaches not lucky enough to be able to make a living out of the game of football, who had to hold down other employment.

Now, at last, I could concentrate solely on what I loved and see if I could make a success of myself in management as I believed I could.

THE ROAD TO SUCCESS

WORKING UNDER DANNY Bergara was a novel experience to say the least. He didn't so much have a screw loose as most of them missing. The first thing he taught me was how to make cheese on toast and how to clean a toilet. He used to carry dirt around in his pocket so that when the YTS kids had finished cleaning too early, in his opinion, he'd throw some on the floor and ask them to clean it up. I thought it was somewhat strange, but it was just Danny's way.

I had six wonderful seasons at Stockport. Within days of me joining, although I had little or nothing to do with it, they got promoted from the old Fourth Division, which obviously created a special buzz around the place and rubbed off on everyone, not least me. Around six months later, Danny asked me whether I wanted to become first-team coach. I must have been doing something right, though in truth, I had got frustrated working with the kids and was chomping at the bit for the opportunity to work with senior players. The youth players couldn't do the things I wanted them to do with the ball. I guess I had been spoilt as a player and the Stockport apprentices were not up to the same standard.

Becoming first-team coach was a breath of fresh air and I guess that was the moment my managerial career took off. I still had to get my full badge, the one you have to get before the pro licence, but after just three days on the course I walked out of the exam room. To me it was a total farce, one big joke – all theory, without any bearing on how you relate to players on a daily basis. One of the FA coaches, Mick Wadsworth, had a right go at me and forced me to go back the following year and finish it off. I'm pleased I did given how the next few months would unfold. Having the qualification is now a prerequisite for working at the top level of the industry.

Danny Bergara always had a problem with the Stockport chairman, Brendan Elwood. Although he lived in Sheffield, Danny had digs opposite the ground, paid for by the club at £21 a month. After several years, the chairman thought it about time Danny bought a house in the area instead of receiving the digs money. As a result there was a frisson of tension between them which reached a crescendo one night in March 1995 at a Miss Stockport County competition. Like everyone else invited, I attended the dinner, but because I was driving I just had a couple of lemonades and left early to get home to Southport where we were still living.

In the early hours of the morning, I guess it must have been around 6am, I got a phone call from John Sainty, the Assistant Manager, saying that Danny had had a fight with the chairman. All hell had apparently broken loose. When I went in the following day, I learned more about what had happened. Danny had had too much to drink and a spat with the chairman ensued, with Danny calling the police to try and get his boss arrested. Not a very clever way of operating. Danny thought he knew what the consequences might be. He told me the chairman would be sending him on a fortnight's holiday and that I'd be taking over until he got back. It was about halfway through the season and I'm thinking to myself, 'Wait a moment. You've tried to get the chairman arrested and you think he's going to send you on a holiday. I don't think so!'

Danny spent all morning in with the board. Then I got a call to go in to see the chairman and when I came out and went back to Danny's office, I witnessed one of the saddest things I have ever seen in football – Danny clearing his office. He had been sacked and was clearly in turmoil. I stood and watched him as he'd take something off his desk, put it in a box, then change his mind and put it back on the desk again, then put it back in the box. This went on for what felt like hours on end and I could feel his pain. Danny knew they had long been priming me to take over, whether it be at the end of that season or in a year or so. Danny was going to move upstairs, at least that was the initial plan, but the bust-up had brought everything forward.

Now Danny enjoyed his whisky. It was a stone's throw from his office to his digs and he used to spend whole nights in the former watching TV and knocking back the booze. Sometimes I'd get phone calls from him about three or four in the morning asking me for needless help. 'The television has broken down' was one frequent line. It wouldn't come on.

"Well, is it plugged in?" I'd ask.

"I'll just go to have a look," came the reply. It wasn't.

Another time he called me in the middle of the night to tell me the game the following day was off.

"It's three in the morning, how do you know?" I said.

"Listen," he said and I could hear the sound of him banging his mobile phone on the frozen pitch outside!

John Sainty and I basically looked after Danny for his final 18 months when he was drinking about a bottle of whisky a day, but what I badly want you to know is that he was fantastic with my family. When Chloe had a bad funfair accident at the age of five, Danny was a saint. I may as well tell you about that incident now since it will give you an idea of the kind of adversity that befell our family well before the child abuse case. I had taken my YTS players to a youth tournament in Crewe – it was in the August not long after I started at Stockport – and I called Ann straight afterwards to let her know I was on my way home. When I couldn't get hold of her, I rang our son Lea and he told me that Chloe had been in a funfair accident in Formby and that it was serious.

I flew home in the car – and I mean flew. As I came off the Southport bypass, a police car that had been parked in a lay-by chased me for nigh on 10 miles. He only caught up with me as I was pulling into the hospital. I blurted out something along the lines of I didn't know whether my daughter was dead or alive and he just calmed me down and warned me that I didn't want to end up in hospital too. The officer knew who I was and let me off with a stern warning.

Ann:

I was still working at Clarence House at the time and had come home from working nights. Dave's sister and brother-in-law had turned up unexpectedly and were going to the local RAF station where there was a funfair. I was tired and initially said no, but they persuaded me. So I went. I have always hated fairground rides, but they convinced me to go on this thing called Cylone Twist. Danielle was about ten and went in the same carriage as me, while my niece Rebecca, roughly the same age as Danielle, went in the one in front with Chloe. As it started to go round, I felt it was going out of control because it went faster and faster with everyone being shoved this way and that. We tried to scream to the guys who were operating it, but they had their backs to the ride and weren't even watching.

The next thing I remember was seeing Chloe fly through the air right past me. She was wearing a multi-coloured little skirt and I knew immediately it was her. People were desperately trying to get the operators to turn the ride off, but they weren't aware anything was wrong. By the time the ride finally stopped, we were all dizzy, not knowing where Chloe was. When I eventually got to her, fearing the worst, she lifted up her head and said, "Mummy, my leg hurts." I knew then she was at least alive. Her upper body was fine, but she'd shattered a femur and broken her pelvis.

She had to have all sorts of scans and was in hospital a full three months, which was hell on the family. For the first month I slept in the hospital with Chloe while Dave had just started full-time in football again and needed to make a go of it. It was a total nightmare. Even after she came out, Chloe kept having to go back to hospital for two or three months every year until she was about 14. I remember one year in particular. No sooner had Chloe come out than Georgia, 20 months old at the time, took seriously ill. After two weeks they diagnosed osteomyelitis and she too was hospitalised for a month. It was an awful time for all of us, but throughout all this time, Danny Bergara and his wife could not have been more sympathetic and generous and I will always have fond memories of how they treated us.

Dave:

Eccentric he certainly was, but I learned a lot from Danny, even if a lot of it was what *not* to do rather than what *to* do. Having said that, he had taken the club forward in leaps and bounds and seeing it happen as first team coach for a couple of years had been a great grounding for me. Whatever Danny thought of Mr. Elwood, I had great respect for him so when I sat down with him to discuss my salary as manager of the club, I didn't anticipate any misunderstandings. Greedy as it may sound, I told him I wanted more than he had been paying me over the previous four years which, quite frankly, had been totally crap.

"But I thought that's the amount you were happy with since that's what Danny kept telling us," he replied. Well you've got to laugh, haven't you? Here I was arguing with a chairman I respect hugely because of something Danny had told him.

We resolved it and my first game in charge was a match against Shrewsbury. It soon became clear the fans had mixed feelings about the managerial change, some singing Danny's name and some mine, but there wasn't long to go until the season ended and the summer calmed all that down.

In my first full season as manager, with John Sainty as my assistant, I basically got to know my team, getting rid of a lot of players and deciding what was needed. We did okay, nothing fantastic, finishing mid-table in the Second Division. But the second year, 1996/97, was totally different. What a time it was. I had built the squad I wanted and we got to the semi-finals of the League Cup, the fourth round of the FA Cup and, most importantly of all, won promotion to Division One, the equivalent of the Championship. Heady days indeed.

In the cup games we didn't have the best of luck overall. In the League Cup semi-final against Middlesbrough we were the better side in the first leg at home, even though our visitors were two divisions higher than us. But Boro scored two late goals against the run of play after their keeper, Mark Schwarzer, kept them in the game on his debut. The tie was effectively over when Fabrizio Ravanelli netted their second in the dying seconds. Or so everyone thought. Credit to my players as they started the second leg brilliantly and right-back Sean Connelly scored early on to give us a chance, his first professional goal. We gave everything we had in atempting to nick an unlikely second, but Tony Dinning's sending off with a quarter of an hour left set the seal on it.

In the FA Cup Birmingham beat us 3-1, Steve Bruce ran the game, or at least in my opinion the referee let him. I was going mad on the touchline, but could do nothing to affect the result.

My team was full of waifs and strays. That's the art of building a side with no budget. I found a bunch of players that other clubs didn't want. Every manager always thinks he can get more out of somebody and I was no exception. Chris Marsden, a midfielder who was kicked out of Notts County because he was considered a bad apple, did tremendously for me – and of course later went on to play for me in the Premiership with Southampton. Brett Angell, a 'misfit' striker who I brought back to the club from Sunderland, was washed out mentally. He'd previously had the number nine shirt at Everton, which is the worst number you could ever wear there. I knew what pressure that brought. Whoever wore that shirt at Everton was looked upon as the best player at the club. Brett just wanted to be liked when he came to Stockport and did an unbelievable job. Then there was Paul Jones, the goalkeeper. I picked him up from Wolves for £40,000, which was a miracle in itself, getting that much money out of the chairman for a club of our size. Paul went on to have a long career of distinction, winning 50 caps for Wales.

The camaraderie amongst the boys was something else, but there were also moments of tragedy. In the early hours of one particular morning early in the season I took a phone call from our captain Mike Flynn saying he couldn't come into training the following day. When I asked why, he told me his mother-in-law had been involved in stabbing his father-in-law to death. I took him and his family out of the media spotlight and put them in a hotel. Mike was a great club captain and went on to play a vital role in our promotion push, somehow managing to put the tragedy behind him. It was on these kind of experiences that I was able to draw when misfortune visited me later.

The League Cup semi-final against Middlesbrough was pure Roy of the Rovers stuff and propelled me into the public eye as an up-and-coming manager. We were flying, had doubled our crowd, and had beaten three Premiership sides – Blackburn away, West Ham at home in front of the television cameras, and then Southampton at the Dell in a replay – to reach the last four of a major cup competition for the first time in Stockport's history. I had a fantastic bunch of players, most of whom were good enough individually to play in the Premiership – and several, like Lee Todd and Alan Armstrong, went on to do so. In the second leg, with the odds stacked against us, it was gut-wrenching to lose so narrowly on aggregate, especially because we missed a great chance in the last minute to equalise. You should have seen Bryan Robson's face: he was crapping himself.

It was a roller-coaster of a season and we were all in it together. Every club I've been at, what the players feel, I feel. That's the way I run a club. I also have a particular way of structuring a football club – I build a team off the field first. They need to know how I work, what my moods are. If I don't go in for a day, I have to be able to trust them. That's how it was at Stockport. As the season progressed, we were playing three games a week sometimes to catch up on league fixtures we'd missed out on playing because of our progress in the cups. I remember being on the bus going to places like Exeter and Plymouth and the players were absolutely shattered.

But to cap a wonderful season, we clinched automatic promotion in the last but one game at Chesterfield. Brett Angell scored the all-important goal, his 19th of the season. Not bad for a 'washed up' striker. The whole season was incredible really, especially given the fact that we had got off to a slow start.

John Sainty was a nervous watcher, even at the best of times. During the Chesterfield game, we were leading 1-0 and I asked Saint how long there was to go. I didn't get a reply, so I asked again, casting the question over my shoulder from my usual position at the side of the pitch. When I turned round, he was leaning against a wall puffing and panting. He just couldn't watch!

We held on and on the way home a celebrating group of fans stopped the team bus outside a pub, so we decided to go in and have a few drinks with them. When we got back to the ground and packed the players off to go and continue their celebrations elsewhere, Saint and I just got absolutely smashed out of our brains drinking champagne. I never made it home that night, sleeping, if you can call it that, in my office.

Bury went up automatically with us and the following day Mr. Elwood came to see me and told me he had to sort my contract out.

"Ay," I said, "and now you've got to pay me what I'm worth."

He said it wasn't a problem and he returned a short time later with two envelopes, one for me and one for John. When I opened mine, the first thought that came into my head was "he's having a laugh." John opens his and shouts "I'll sign it now."

Well you can guess what had happened. The chairman, who had a slight stutter, had given us both the wrong envelope!

"Give me a pen," said John. "Ner-ner-ner-no," replied the embarrassed chairman, desperately trying to get the words out. Even when the envelopes were switched round, I still couldn't sign.

"Well how much are you looking for?" asked the chairman. Quite frankly I didn't know. I had discussed a figure with Ann, but I didn't feel I could tell Mr. Elwood, for whom I had so much time, who had bent over backwards to get me players he often couldn't afford and who always let me manage without interfering.

About a week later he invited me to lunch at a local hotel and I decided I'd give him the figure I had in mind. Let's just say I asked him for a third more than I was getting at the time, so it was a massive hike – but without any hesitation he stretched out his hand and said "done".

I cheekily asked whether that meant if I'd have asked for even more I'd have got it. "No," he replied. "But if you'd have asked for less, I'd have been disappointed."

With our heads in the clouds, Ann and I went off to Spain on a well-deserved holiday with our three girls. Just after we got there, I received a phone call from Jonathan Barnett, the agent, to tell me that Rupert Lowe, the Southampton Chairman, was after me.

"Who does he want?" I asked, assuming Rupert was after one of my players.

"You, you daft bat," said Jonathan. "Oh and by the way we are on a conference call with Rupert now. . ." It was an interesting way to begin a relationship with a new chairman.

So, no sooner had I arrived in Spain than I flew straight back to meet Rupert, but not before calling John Sainty to ask him to come with me.

I told Rupert how much admiration I had for my chairman at Stockport and that I needed him to be told Southampton wanted me without giving him the impression that I had already been approached. I suppose in one way I should not have spoken to Lowe to start with, but there was no way I would just walk out of Stockport. I had just signed a generous new contract after leading the club to their first promotion to the second tier of football in 60 years. It was only right that the two chairmen did business together and, preferably, while I was on holiday in Spain. So I agreed everything with Rupert and returned to Ann for our holiday. It wasn't long before Brendon Elwood called me to say he'd had an inquiry from Southampton. I felt it only right at that point to tell Mr Elwood that I'd already spoken to Lowe. He wasn't angry and said it was a fantastic opportunity, but he also said he'd match whatever wages Southampton were offering me. I replied that I'd turn down whatever figure he came up with because this was the Premiership. This was where I had always dreamed of managing.

"Good," he said with a certain amount of relief. "If you'd have said yes, I don't know how the hell I could have paid you the same amount!"

I was very pleased to be leaving Stockport on good terms and in a better position than when I took over. That's something I think has been true at all of my clubs. It's important to me in how I conduct myself in the business of our sport, which is full of charlatans and people who do not keep their word. I'm not naïve – in fact far from it – and I don't wear rose-tinted spectacles, but I do have a strong sense of what is right and wrong and I fight hard for that both on my own behalf and also my players'.

The next time I met Rupert was at his home to finalise personal terms. I only had a little Ford as a club car at Stockport, so just to impress him, I rang a mate who had a swish Jaguar and asked if I could borrow it for the day. While I was having contract talks with Rupert, he looked out of the window and said that the club would give me a car to the standard I was used to. Result.

SAINTS ALIVE

IT WON'T BE a surprise to you to learn that much of the football head-lines that appear in national newspapers are what I could charitably call 'speculation'. A less charitable person might call them deliberate false-hoods or plain old lies. The problem is these headlines are presented as facts and often when they are wrong they cause people in the game problems. For example, you can imagine my surprise, whilst back on holiday in Spain, when the *Daily Mirror* splashed the news that David Platt had been given the Southampton job. They had got the right Chris-tian name but not the right surname! Typical . . .

My first game as manager of Saints was memorable for many reasons. It was August 1997, and we were playing Bolton at home. I was full of anticipation for the task ahead. As seemed to happen every year, pretty much every pundit or 'expert' was tipping my new club for rele-gation. As I got out of my car, three people from SISA (Southampton Independent Supporters Association) walked up to me and told me in no uncertain terms that if I didn't play 'Le God', otherwise known as Matt Le Tissier, they'd get of rid of me like they'd got rid of every other manager. Not 'welcome, Dave' or 'good luck, Dave', just a full frontal assault telling me how to do my job.

It took me aback and I reacted, asking them if that was a threat — because if it was, I'd get two double decker bus loads of Scousers down there to sort them out. I didn't even know who these people were and yet they thought they had a big say in what went on at Southampton — as I later discovered.

The players had told me early on in pre-season training that they had thought they would go down the previous season under Graeme Souness. It was an oldish team that needed rebuilding and that's what I set about doing, even though I knew it would be incredibly difficult on the small budget I was given by Premier League standards. It didn't worry me too much because it was a lot bigger than what I'd been given at Stockport.

Let me say straight away I never had a problem with Le Tissier. He was probably the most gifted footballer I've ever had the pleasure of being involved with. He could do things with the ball that you just had to stand back and applaud. You could see why he was such a God amongst Saints fans. But the problem was nothing was ever short. You'd only see Tiss hit a raking 40-yard pass on the button. He was a lovely man, but he also did like his hamburgers too much. He had everything you want in a player, but I had to ask the question if Matt himself actually wanted it badly enough. I always felt with Tiss, he liked his lot too much, a big fish in a little pond. Given his talent Tiss should have plied his trade at a bigger club than Southampton. Rumours were rife that Spurs bid for him around that time, but I can confirm that never happened. Chelsea were apparently interested, but also never made a formal bid. A lot of managers I spoke to at the time thought he was a liability, but he was so gifted. Ideal for Southampton in a way — loved by the fans and players and I loved him too. But there comes a time in your management career where you have to make a decision. Around Christmas I felt he just wasn't pulling his weight. I know a lot has been made of the fact that I was the manager who, in January 1998, dropped Le Tissier. It was the first time in four years and only the second occasion in Matt's 12 remarkable years at The Dell that this had happened to him, but it was for one reason and one reason alone — he wasn't delivering the goods.

I remember being hammered by a supporter close to the dugout for dropping 'Le God', yet a few days later, when I had to bring Matt back because of other injuries in the squad, the same fan started slaughtering me for not taking him off when he was clearly struggling for fitness. Can't win sometimes, can you? I firmly believe that if I'd kept playing Tiss, we'd have lost more games than we won.

Despite losing seven out of the first nine Premier League games, in my first full season we finished 11th, five places better than the previous campaign. For me that was a fantastic first season in the top flight. The second was about getting younger players in at the price we could afford. The likes of Le Tissier were coming to the end. Ken Monkou was another. I brought in David Hirst, Carlton Palmer, Stuart Ripley and, later, thanks to a recommendation from then Latvia national manager Gary Johnson, Marian Pahars. Even then the season didn't start very well – two points from the first eight games, just like Tottenham performed in 2008/09 under Juande Ramos, who paid with his job. The difference was, I was at a developing team that perennially struggled, so the expectation was so much less. The new players gradually started bedding in and finding their feet. To help the large number of new additions to the squad all gel, I took them and the wives and girl-friends away pre-season to La Manga just like Jim Smith used to do at Derby. Method in my madness: wives there, lads behave. Also, I always feel that if the wives and girlfriends are settled, so are the players. Far better than having them moan about not knowing anyone and not being able to find the right schools for the kids and things like that. There are so many factors that go into buying a player and making them successful at your club which is all brand new to them and their family. All of them need a settling in period. If any manager gets a player who does the business from day one, he's lucky. So I always knew the process of assimilating all the new players would take a while and was prepared for a short term blip for the longer term gain. Thankfully I was right and managed to keep Saints up: I believed in my ability and the fact that I'd get them out of it. If you're losing games and you know the players aren't good enough, you're waiting for relegation. But I had players I knew were good enough. All they needed was belief and bit of luck.

Even though the 1998/99 season was one long struggle, I never for once considered deviating from the road I was on. Did I think I might get sacked? No. Was there any indication of that from the board? Again, no. Because we'd done so well the year before, the expectations had risen a bit, but ultimately this was Southampton and they were used to perenially struggling against relegation. Fans always think they can do better than the man in the hot seat, but the majority of them, because they'd had years of battling against the big boys, didn't put too much pressure on me. In fact when I joined the club, Lawrie McMenemy – the manager who had won the FA Cup and promotion to the First Division for the club in the mid-1970s – told me that finishing fourth from bottom constituted success. That was exactly where we finished, one position above relegation, but it was not how I saw things. My aim was to finish top. I knew quite well I couldn't do it, but if I didn't finish top, I'd want to finish second. And if not second, then third, etc. If you think like McMenemy, invariably you finish even lower. So I set my sights high. People may say that's stupid, but that was my philosophy from day one.

We loved it, the whole family did, at Southampton. I loved the club and everything about it. I remain convinced to this day that if the court case hadn't have intervened, I'd have kept them in the Premier League. No-one can say I didn't make progress. Southampton bought Kevin Davies for £500,000 roughly three months before I arrived. I sold him for £7.5m, then got him back again for virtually nothing from Blackburn when I swapped him for Egil Ostenstad. As part of the initial deal to sell Davies to Blackburn I signed a young England Under-21 striker called James Beattie. Beattie went on to score 68 goals in 204 games for Southampton before he became Everton's £6m record signing in January 2005. I also added Dean Richards for nothing from Wolves in July 1999 and the club sold him to Tottenham for around £8m two years later.

I'VE ALREADY MENTIONED the then Southampton Chairman Rupert Lowe and his name will come up several times more in the book. Rupert and I could not have been more different in terms of personality and upbringing, but you know what, I got on really well with him. I even used to go shooting with him from time to time. Just how different we were was illustrated on that La Manga pre-season trip. All the staff went to dinner one night and discussed what we used to do as kids to earn pocket money. I said I did a milk round. Terry Cooper, one of the coaches, said he used to pick potatoes, to which Rupert replied, "so did I Terry, I used to drive the tractor." That summed Rupert up: he loved to think he was one of the boys, but was far more of a patrician figure than the management team and players. He had been educated at an exclusive prep school in Oxford and then went on to the equally exclusive Radley public school before enjoying a successful business career that included working as a futures trader at Morgan Grenfell, the investment bank, and its later owner Deutsche Bank. Hockey was his preferred sport and I felt he was not really steeped in football tradition – not that that was a problem at all. He will doubtless deny this, but he was also prone to what I felt was exaggeration at the time I worked for him – although I realise that many Saints fans, and others, will think that never changed. Even at the start of the 2008/09 season, when I phoned him in my capacity as Cardiff City manager to enquire about a player – I won't say who – he replied that Southampton were going to "burn up this division" with the kids they had. What happened? Saints were relegated after struggling all season and eventually went into administration due to financial problems and earned a ten point deduction effective from the start of the 2009/10 season. Many might think it strange, but, in truth, I still have a lot of time for Rupert as a person.

I have got on, in fact, with all the chairmen I've worked for – even Sir Jack Hayward at Wolves, who I will come to later on. It was only when Sir Jack started to believe outside influences, as Rupert did at Southampton, that we drifted apart. Things like supporter message boards, the worst thing ever invented, began to have influence at this time, the turn of the century. Who on earth uses them? More often than not, lonely people still living with their parents with nothing better to do than sit by a computer and write rubbish. Many of them don't even go to games. Players read message boards, even though I've always told mine not to. They have a lot of spare time on their hands and often take a peek. In my opinion some of the ridiculous stuff that's on there can end up seriously damaging players mentally.

We had a fabulous home while I was at Saints and had felt almost from day one that this was the right place to live, even though our Scouse accents probably seemed a bit out of place in the middle of Hampshire. The girls had adapted brilliantly and set up a strong network of friends. Professionally too, this was where I had always wanted to be, among the top 20 football managers in the country. Southampton had limited resources compared to many Premiership clubs and my brief from Rupert Lowe was simply to keep the club up, then build for the future with younger players. I believe I achieved this. Don't forget, the season before I went they had avoided the drop by the skin of their teeth. I know our form dipped in 1998/99 compared to the previous season and we avoided relegation late on, but as I have said, new players had been bedding in and that takes time. And I mean time. We had a five-year plan, not two years.

I had kept telling the press there was a long way to go. Despite what the statistics might imply, you are never relegated in December when many were writing us off because we were 19th, one point off the bottom, despite the fact we were also only three points behind Coventry in 17th. Nevertheless it was not a comfortable situation having to win our last three games of the season to ensure survival. It was kind of poetic that it was Everton, my hometown club, whom we beat 2-0 on that final day to save our status. In a way, although I set my sights higher than that, you had to say that was a great achievement since so many people never thought we'd could stay up.

I know that when I found myself out of the picture five months into the following season we were not that much better off in terms of league position, but the rebuilding was still going on. As I say, you don't build over one season without money. I feel – and always felt – that Rupert came under pressure from a certain section of the crowd and other influences when he took the decision to put me on gardening leave, which, to me, felt like I was being got rid of. I wasn't the first manager to be sidelined with the team struggling near the bottom, and history has shown that I certainly wasn't the last.

I honestly think I'd still be at the club today if circumstances had been different. I was in the job for the long term, even in the modern environment when managers seem to be chopped and changed every five minutes. Southampton were among the clubs who believed in continuity if they could find stability. And it works. Alan Curbishley, after all, stayed at Charlton for 15 years and David Moyes, the LMA's 2008/09 Manager of the Season, has been at Everton for almost a decade. Who knows how far I could have taken Southampton if I'd been given the chance? What I firmly believe would never have happened under me is relegation from the Premier League, which finally visited the club in 2005. I can promise you that, however close we might have come in my last full season there, I would have kept us up.

I have a developed a reputation for building teams up from scratch with little money to spend. But I never got a chance to finish the job at Southampton. Fate was about to intervene.

THE NIGHTMARE BEGINS

AS I WATCHED the players celebrating staving off relegation at the end of the 1998/99 season, following that 2-0 win over Everton at the Dell, I allowed myself a little thought about how hard I had worked to get to this moment. I was on the crest of a wave, exactly where I wanted to be. Then my thoughts switched immediately to the coming season. The mayhem of jubilation shared by players and supporters alike washed over me. I think it's the same for any manager. Once one season closes you immediately begin planning for the next one. You can never switch off.

Little did I realise that the test which awaited me had nothing to do with football, although unwittingly the first indication had crossed my path.

Before the end of the season, Ann and I had received separate letters from the police asking us if we were aware of anything untoward that had happened while we were working at Clarence House. It was one of those standard letters with your name filled in at the top. I wrote back and said I had not seen anything that was either unprofessional or unacceptable. Ann wrote back and said the same. Then, a month or so later, I received a letter from a solicitor asking me to comment on a man called Michael Lawson, who had worked at the school. I responded that in my experience he was a conscientious worker. I received no reply. As you can imagine with a relegation run in to oversee, letters like that were hardly on my priority list. As a manager you deal with so much mail – fans praising you, fans slagging you off, fans telling you which players to pick and not to pick – that you deal with the correspondence as quickly and effectively as you can and get on with your job as you see fit.

A friend of mine used to say that when things are going really well, watch out because there is always something lurking round the corner to ruin them. They also say that trouble comes in threes. I was about to see both maxims proved true.

Our cocoon of happiness had already been shattered in March when Ann's 21-year-old nephew, Graham Neale, her brother's son, died of a brain tumour. Then my brother-in-law, Peter, the husband of Ann's sister Dot, was tragically killed. He was working on some railway lines when he was hit by a train. The whole family had to live through this terrible time and the ensuing investigation into Peter's death. Peter was more than just a brother-in-law, he was loved by everyone and even taught me to drive.

You can imagine, then, our doubt about leaving for an already booked holiday in the United States. We only decided to go ahead when Ann's sister told us no date had been set for Peter's funeral. That was all traumatic enough. Little did I know that my own personal nightmare was about to unfold.

We returned home after a wonderful break two weeks later just before the date which was now set for Peter's funeral, 14 June. As we got off the plane at Gatwick just after dawn following one of those sleepless overnight flights from America, our only thought was to get to St. Helens, where Dot lived. Because we had not been sure, while we were away, exactly when Peter's funeral would be, we had left the appropriate clothing in the back of the car and were quickly on our way north, battling against fatigue, both mental and physical. As we drove I checked my voicemail for messages. I heard my secretary's voice and assumed it might be good news. Perhaps the chairman had agreed to give me untold millions to strengthen the squad. I called in as she requested and Daphne told me that Merseyside police wanted to speak to me. Strange. I had only ever been in trouble with the law over a couple of minor speeding offences, had never even been in a police station before and wondered what it could be about. I thought it could only be a follow-up to the letter about Michael Lawson. Ann was more suspicious as she could not work out why the police didn't want to talk to her as well. After all she'd been a colleague of Lawson and had also been sent the same letter as me.

I made the call to a DC Curran from the car as we drove northwards with the three girls asleep in the back. I got through straight away, introduced myself and told DC Curran I was on my way to Liverpool for a family funeral.

"Yes," he replied. "We know."

How did he know? Despite this unnerving response and my wife's suspicions, I remained relatively unconcerned and put it to the back of my mind, especially since DC Curran had told me he was looking for mere historical evidence, there was no special urgency and that he could come down to Southampton to see me if necessary. In that case, I reasoned, it couldn't be that important could it? We agreed to meet the day after Peter's funeral, which had been made quite public because of the circumstances of his death.

We duly attended the funeral without mentioning to anyone that I had to see the police the following day. As I reflect on that terrible sequence of events, I remain convinced that they had planned to catch me when I was emotionally at my lowest point – in the immediate aftermath of a family funeral soaked in sadness for Peter, who died far too young.

Despite her fragile emotional state, Ann insisted on coming with me to the police station and I couldn't see why not. Of course, we had to tell a whole lot of white lies, not only to our girls, but to Ann's sister who was understandably in a terrible state anyway, saying something about how I had to meet my bank manager. What was the point of telling them the real reason? After all, a couple of minutes in the police station and I'd be on my way, having helped serve the cause of justice. Done and dusted.

When we arrived at Wavertree Road police station, the two officers, DCs Curran and Thomas, who to my footballing mind looked like a couple of old-fashioned strikers – one big, one small – told us that Ann was not allowed to be in the room with me since they were going to ask me some questions about Operation Care (Child Abuse Residential Establishments), the police operation to hunt down those guilty of child abuse in Merseyside child care homes.

Ann:

As I drove away from the police station, I felt sick to my stomach. I could sense something was very wrong. I stopped and sobbed down the phone to Dina Nixon, a child protection officer whom we'd worked with at Clarence House and who had become one of our dearest friends. In fact we had stayed the night at their house after the funeral. She and her husband John later helped us tirelessly in the build-up to Dave's trial, putting us up as we regularly used to stay over on a Saturday night, pouring over every statement, sometimes until two or three in the morning.

Dina came straight into town to meet me at a cafe and tried to calm me down, before taking me back to her house to await Dave's call. I told her I had long been concerned that the police, who we knew were deep into a series of investigations into child abuse across the country, and in particular on Merseyside, might be looking for a 'big fish' like Dave.

Dave:

I could see the look of panic on Ann's face as she drove off. I didn't want to leave her alone, or she me, but they left us with no choice. I was alone and before I knew it I was being accused of the most hateful crime I can imagine – abusing children who had been in my care.

DC Thomas sat me down and informed me of the allegations which had been made against me. The accusations, he said, in what felt to me an almost triumphant tone, involved sexual and physical abuse which, if proven, could lead to imprisonment. In fact, I was under arrest pending a full investigation.

That's when my head began to whirl crazily.

Next they told me the name of the person who had accused me. This lad was a young adult by now and said I had sexually abused him while at Clarence House. I did not recognise his name at all and had no recollection of who he was. I could not create a mental picture of him, no matter how hard I tried. Something was very wrong. Here I was, thinking that the police just wanted to question me briefly, establish what a load of lies they had been told and that would be the end of it. Now I stood accused of the most abominable crime I could imagine.

At that point I asked if I could have a lawyer, and I called Terry McGraw, the solicitor we had used when we moved house. He promised to get someone there within the hour. While I waited, the desk sergeant, who seemed genuinely embarrassed that I was there, gave me the newspapers to read and a cup of tea. But the officers weren't all like him and everyone, of course, knew who I was.

I tried to read the papers, but, just as the room was a blur, so were the words in the paper. I stared at the print, unable to take anything in. All that whirred around in my head was one unanswerable question, 'How am I supposed to explain all this to my wife, my three elder children and my little four-year-old, to my mum and dad, brother and sister? What words do I use? How will people in the football world react to hearing the news?'

As I looked through the pages of the paper I began to envisage the headlines about me superimposed upon it. They didn't make pretty reading and I realised that this would be big news. In fact, if it got out, the press would tear me to shreds. I tried to blank that out of my mind, but the question kept on nagging away at me. Surely no-one would actually believe all this? Could they? What chance would I have if people believed these lies? My thoughts were on a loop, going round and round. I could not escape them. It was mental torture. The nightmare had begun.

I was shaken out of those depressing thoughts by the door opening and the solicitor walking in. The first thing he said to me was "Hiya Dave, I'm a red nose!" Meaning, of course, he was a Liverpool fan. That touch of humour lightened the atmosphere a bit, but the two police officers didn't appreciate it at all. I felt their attitude was sarcastic and belittling. When they began the questioning again and I protested that I had children of my own, one of them turned to me and said, with a horrible smirk on his face, "That doesn't mean you haven't done anything. We've just sent someone down who said exactly the same thing, and we've put him away for seven years."

I sat in stunned disbelief, unable to contemplate that anyone could possibly imagine I was a criminal, especially when my alleged crime involved such sickening offences. In so many ways it was the worst allegation that they could possibly have been thrown at me. The accusation that I had physically abused a child was bad enough, but being accused of sexually abusing children to me is the most awful crime imaginable, the most evil crime anyone could commit. I felt both humiliated and angry. None of it made sense to me, they had indeed caught me at a low emotional ebb and even to this day I remember at one point thinking, 'I would prefer to be falsely accused of murder.'

I half-wondered whether Jeremy Beadle was going to suddenly jump out as part of one of those TV stitch-ups.

"Is this some sort of joke?" I blurted out. Their response, if I recall correctly, was merely to write down what I said as evidence.

I knew that I needed to get out of this horrendous place and back to Ann. Instead the police's questions came thick and fast. Despite my anger, I answered everything, knowing that lack of cooperation could potentially count against me.

Did I know the person who had accused me?

"No, never heard of him."

Had I ever abused him?

"No."

Did I ever have a red car?

"No, I have never owned a red car."

"Are you sure, sir?" they asked repeatedly. The person accusing me had stated that I had tried to strangle him until he choked and that I had sexually abused him in a red car.

"Red?" I responded. "Hardly likely, I'm an Evertonian."

They didn't get it.

It went on and on, driving me to distraction and I found it very hard to keep my cool. It was all so outrageous.

When the officers had exhausted their questions, I was told they would let me know what happened next, and they promised that the press would not be informed. They would have no knowledge of anything because I had not been charged. I was simply, as they say, helping police with their inquiries. I was released and asked to return in September, three months later.

While still inside the station, I immediately rang Ann at Dina's. I will never forget that phone call. Ann went silent when I told her I had been arrested, but then she screamed and threw the phone across the room, before breaking down.

Ann:
I was horrified. I knew what this meant. I could see how the nightmare scenario would unfold, but even then I wasn't close to how bad it would actually prove to be.

Dave:
As Ann sobbed, I told her to stay calm, that it was all a pack of lies and that nothing would come out of it. Our privacy would be respected because the press were not going to be told.

Fat chance. As I left the station, two reporters were skulking outside. They were not even meant to know I was there. The only people who knew I was at Wavertree Road police station were Ann, Dina, my solicitor, the police and me. You don't have to be Einstein to work out how the press found out. The pair of them stared at me, but did not ask any questions. It was pretty clear, though, that the circus would soon to be coming to town. As much as anything I think it was the police's way of unnerving me and of showing me that from now on, there would be no hiding place. My question to them was, what did I have to hide from?

As I drove off for the 30-minute journey to Dina's, all I could think of was my family. I had to speak to them and let them know what was happening. There again, there were some things I had been accused of that were so disgusting I couldn't even tell Ann, even though she bombarded me with questions as we walked around Dina's garden when

I arrived. I played it all down, genuinely thinking in my stunned state that it would all blow over. "You're so naïve," Ann kept saying, because she understood that I was the one who was holding the case together. Some people who had worked with me at Clarence House already had been arrested and had trial dates, she said. It later transpired that two of them were sent down, only to be acquitted at retrial, following the breakdown of my own trial. Ann was convinced that because of who I was, the police were trying to use me as a high profile example to get as many convictions as possible.

Having discussed who needed to be phoned and told about what was going on, first of all I called Rupert Lowe. To be fair to him, Rupert was pretty good about it once he learned what had happened. One humiliating call could have turned into another, but I did not want too many other people to know at this stage. I was conscious that Ann's sister, who was getting over the death of her husband, still believed I had gone to see the bank manager. At least that's what we thought. As it happened, she had twigged that it was more important and when we told her she went absolutely bonkers. Her life must have seemed pretty bleak right at that moment in so many ways. I couldn't help but feel for her, even though this nightmare was happening to me.

Once I had made the few necessary calls, it may seem odd, but I was consumed with a sense of relief. I think I assumed the worst was over. I have never really been afraid of much in my life, but making those calls was one of the scariest things I have ever had to do. But it had renewed my confidence and now I had convinced myself that the police would surely come down on the side of a person who had never committed a single crime and obviously would realise that this whole thing was a farce.

I had calmed down and it just seemed so obvious to me that the accusation against me was a lie and that someone was trying it on. Even though I had just gone through a thoroughly degrading process, at this stage I bore no animosity towards the police at all. They were only doing their job, after all. If someone is accused of being a paedophile, of course they have to be questioned. Children have to be protected. The police had, in general, been polite towards me, although the press being informed when I had been specifically told they wouldn't be did really nark me.

As a football manager you become adept at reading body language when you talk to players. My assessment of the two officers' body language in that interview room was that 'we know this isn't right, Mr. Jones, but you have to understand we have to ask these questions.' They had to check it out, of course they did.

How wrong I was.

I had now convinved myself that this hideous situation was such a huge and obvious mistake that it would all blow over very quickly. It just hadn't dawned on me yet quite how much, once they get their teeth into you, the police will not let anyone from a high profile, public occupation go when the spotlight falls on them.

I was at an advantage because I knew the allegations were utterly false – I hadn't yet come to understand quite how malicious – but at the same time this placed me at a huge disadvantage as I had no idea how hard I would have to fight, how much it would cost me in so many ways and how deeply this whole process would affect me, causing me to suffer awful abuse from opposing supporters and eventually lose my job as manager of Southampton.

I'm not looking to blame anyone, but I'd love to know exactly who tipped off the press so that I could tell them face to face how that led to untold anguish and agony being heaped upon my family.

THAT NIGHT, ANN and I drove back to Southampton. We had to. My team was beginning pre-season training the next day and I needed to be there. We arrived home late. The first thing I did when I got home was take a shower, I felt dirty and wanted to wash all remnants of my ordeal away. I couldn't sleep, however. I spent the night mentally bracing myself for the whirlwind which I knew was about to be unleashed. I knew I was going to be at the eye of this storm, but I had no conception of how wild and devastating it was going to be.

THE FIRST VICTIM

THE NEXT MORNING was as horrible as it was predictable. Merseyside police released the information that they had arrested a 42-year-old man from the Southampton area. It wasn't difficult for people to put two and two together, especially as those reporters had seen me leave Wavertree Road police station. I had not yet been charged, but the news was blasted all over Sky just the same. Other TV and radio stations soon followed suit. When Ann arrived back home after taking the kids to school, two guys got out of a car and stood in front of her to stop her turning into the drive. She wound the window down to see what they wanted and one of them asked her if she was Mrs. Jones.

Ann:

I knew straight away they were reporters. One of them shouted at me, "I want to speak to you about your husband and child abuse allegations."

I replied that the accusations weren't true and as I tried to drive into the driveway, they banged on the car window. It was horrible. I ran inside as quick as I could and shut the curtains. I was absolutely paranoid. No-one was supposed to know but us and yet the press had arrived outside the house.

I felt so isolated. The children were at school, Dave's mum and dad were on holiday, Dave himself was in training, my son was at work. I could feel all this pressure bearing down on me. I tried to raise Dave, but couldn't get hold of him, as he was out on the pitch taking training. I sat behind the firmly shut curtains and cried.

The next challenge was having to go to Georgia's school to pick her up. I waited for all the parents to collect their kids and then went in to warn her teacher about what was going on. As soon as I began to explain to her that Dave had been arrested, I just dissolved. My biggest worry was what her reaction would be. She was taken aback, but also very sympathetic and put her arm round me to give me some comfort. When I left the class-room, there was Georgia skipping along merrily with her little red bag, completely unaware of why Mummy was crying. She was still only four after all. I had to pretend I had something in my eye. You can tell little white lies to children of that age.

It was harder for Chloe. She was older and at senior school. She had to be told what was going on, yet had to continue to go to school after her dad had been plastered all over the papers. There was no way we could keep it from her as we realised other kids would soon start on about it and we needed to tell her the truth to make sure she could cope with it all.

Even more importantly, we had to tell Danielle since she worked at a nursery. We had to take into account the parents of children there as well as Danielle's colleagues.

Dave:

Before we could contact him, my son, Lea, heard on the radio that his dad had been arrested and was being accused of paedophilia. That was bad enough, but it was even worse for my parents. They were into the second week of a holiday in Portugal and we had no contact number for them. They were sitting having a drink with one of my brothers and my sister. Sky TV was on in the bar and suddenly a picture of me flashed up on the screen. As a Premier League manager they were fairly used to this on Sky Sports, but this was on the news channel. That concentrated their minds and with the help of the famous Sky ticker they learned the breaking news about their son.

This still hurts me all these years later. Who leaked my name to the press? It had to be a police officer keen to make capital for the force in making this newsworthy allegation public and heap pressure on me, seeking to make me crack and confess, I suppose. It's a dirty tactic that we still see used to this day. In November 2007 the then Portsmouth manager Harry Redknapp's house was raided at dawn. Incredibly the police had with them reporters and photographers from a number of newspapers. How can that be right? Especially when no charges ever followed the search – only headlines.

Whoever it was that released the news about my interrogation could at least have had the common decency to let me speak to my parents first. Dad called me. He wanted to come home straight away. He and mum were both devastated, even though I tried, in my inimitable way, to play it down.

The news spread like a raging bull, bringing with it growing press intrusion, but I am lucky enough to be the kind of person who can compartmentalise things. Always have been. If I've got a problem that won't surface for a while, I put it away until then. I knew I couldn't do anything about this until I returned to see the police again, so I set it to one side.

Ann is totally different: she worried about it. I don't see the point in worrying about something that is out of your control. It drives Ann crazy sometimes. Being how I am, because I knew I was innocent, I just got on with my job. Some people may not have been able to do that, but I could. Ann would want to talk about the allegations more than I did, saying these people were after me for my money and that I should stop being so naïve. I would reply that they were liars and the police would soon see that and that we should put the whole thing to the back of our minds since there was nothing we could do about it. She still thought I was being utterly naïve and told me so. She was right, of course, but I couldn't see it then as I was so convinced my innocence would win through.

The situation could have pushed us away from each other. In fact it did the opposite. It brought us closer together. But the level of intrusion into our lives and those around us was becoming intolerable. I was being accused of abuse yet the only people being abused were me and my family.

It began to take its toll.

My dad fell ill immediately after returning from Portugal. Two days later he went into hospital. You couldn't have chosen a more vulnerable person. Throughout my life, I always believed that if you took an x-ray of dad, you would have found all of his nerves in his stomach. He was suffering from tremendous pain in his abdomen, but they couldn't find anything wrong with him at first and for the best part of ten days was treated by a GP at home. When it became unbearable, he was re-admitted to hospital for tests. He was diagnosed with a burst bowel and shortly afterwards fell into a coma. I remain convinced it was stress-induced, brought on by the shock of learning about the allegations against me the way he did – sceptic shock I think they call it.

My case was actually the last thing we talked about before dad fell unconscious and was placed on a life-support machine. The next time I saw him, he was in intensive care fighting for his life.

As he lay there, motionless, I took to talking to him through the voice in my head. People who have been though this experience will know what I mean. When someone you love is on a life-support machine, for some reason you don't talk aloud. You quietly and slowly say what you have to say. I kept it simple. "It will be okay, dad. I will make sure that everything is okay. Don't worry, things will be fine."

I decided I would do the one thing I could to help. I decided to phone the police and explain how seriously ill my dad was, that we did not know if he would survive. What might help was if he knew the police had seen through the accusations and that my case was closed.

I made the call, explained the situation, and asked them to bring forward my return to the police station. Or if they couldn't do that, at least give me some good news to tell my dad. Fat chance. I was told I had simply to return on schedule.

Worried that the police were showing no signs of believing in me and my innocence, I changed solicitors, engaging Stephen Pollard, from the London firm Kingsley Napley. Stephen was one of the top experts in this area of the law in the country with a tremendous reputation and who I came to trust and respect. We spent long hours going through how best to approach going back to face the police's questions and Stephen showed me how holes could be picked in my story by anyone choosing to disbelieve me, how I had to be very careful about what I said and how I said it, how simply being innocent wasn't necessarily enough.

But before my return trip to Merseyside came the news I was truly dreading. We were all summoned to the hospital and faced with the decision to turn off dad's life support machine. It is a horrific thing to have to do – end the life of someone who brought you into the world and nurtured you – and yet we knew it was the only option. It was devastating. We sat round his bed as the deed was done.

My emotions were in utter turmoil as I asked for some time alone with him. I could not help but feel that his death was because of what was happening to me. Without question his illness had been brought on by learning the way he did of the allegations against me. It struck him down and all I could think of at that moment was that him lying dead in front of me was my fault – and of course the fault of the person or persons unknown who had leaked the news to the media.

I staved off my anger for a moment, kissed dad on the forehead and said, through the voice in my head, "pass in peace, dad. I'll make sure everything turns out okay. I promise."

The problem was I now knew it was a promise I might struggle to keep.

THANK YOU, SIR ALEX

I'M A PRETTY straightforward bloke really. I'm totally absorbed in my love for football and my job, and my family life. That's my world. I understand that being a Premier League manager brings with it pressures, influences and media interest, which many people would see as undesirable, but I believe are simply part of the job.

Even then, I could not believe the maelstrom my life had become since the first public airing of my predicament. It is very difficult for me to explain exactly how tough things were becoming. I was angry and upset about the death of my father – I still carry it with me every day – but right then the feelings were very raw and I wanted to lash out. But I kept my counsel, Ann playing a huge part in simmering me down.

Things were not helped by knowing that huge swathes of people who read about the case would simply leap to the assumption that I was guilty, would believe what they read. I had already learnt that the internet chat rooms, a relatively new phenomenon in 1998, were ablaze with gossip.

I found out later that one guy posted a message that he could tell I was a pervert from having met me years previously when I was a non-league manager. As it happened my brother was monitoring that particular chat room at the time and, after a heated exchange of emails, the guy was forced to admit he had never met me at all. That was just one small example of the kind of thing I was beginning to have to cope with.

Having avoided relegation the previous season, I was determined to keep Saints up again in 1999/2000, and hoped that my long term strategy would begin to bear fruit in terms of moving us up the table and away from the danger zone. Southampton were used to spending the entire season living in the shadow of relegation and we all knew it would be tough, but now I had this new distraction to cope with – not just for me but for everyone associated with the club as well, who were being constantly bombarded with questions from the media about how they or I were coping. I knew that it could become a crutch which would give people a ready-made excuse for failure to perform. I was not going to stand for that.

I needn't have worried about how the players were going to react – suffice to say they did what all footballers do, took the piss. The next day when I went into work, the lads put a white T-shirt up on a peg with arrows on it and a ball and chain. I burst out laughing. It was brilliant.

I was also very grateful that Rupert Lowe and the Southampton board backed me to the hilt. The club issued an immediate statement announcing, 'Dave continues to strongly maintain his innocence and the club will stand by him whilst the legal process takes place.' So far so good – innocent 'til proven guilty. The problem, as I discovered later to my cost, was that the legal process would take some considerable time. Time is not a commodity in which modern football deals in any way.

As the publicity gathered momentum, the next situation I knew I would have to face was a stadium packed with fans on match days – both our own supporters and those from opposing clubs. I expected some would shout abuse at me, but that is part and parcel of being a football manager. Every week in the Premier League you walk out in front of 30, 40, 50, 60,000 people and have to be prepared to take some stick. What I had not been prepared for was people suggesting there was no smoke without fire.

The police clearly didn't think the allegations were unsubstantiated. I attended Wavertree Road police station again alone to learn that a second person who had been at Clarence House had now come forward to accuse me of some fairly hideous offences. I was told that I would be needed again a week later to either be formally charged or released. This was now the stuff of absolute nightmares as I felt as if the sword of Damocles dangled above me on the thinnest of threads. The police clearly believed the witnesses and were choosing not to listen to my protestations. I had been anticipating this turn of events as Stephen, my solicitor, had warned me to expect them to escalate things, and they were clearly doing so, but it was still a stomzch-churning thing to hear.

In the interim football became my solace, my cocoon against the outside world.

The next game was at Manchester United. It had become public knowledge that I would shortly be returning for Liverpool for the pivotal 'will he be charged or not' meeting. I wasn't the only one who was under scrutiny in the papers, however. A woman had gone to the press alleging she had been involved in some sort of liaison with one of my players and that it had involved the use of a chicken leg. God knows what he was meant to be doing with a chicken leg. For a joke, the players secretly ordered a bucket-load of chicken legs to be delivered for lunch and were running around waving them at the team-mate in question. It was a brief moment of collective childishness of the kind that happens in every dressing room. It brought a smile to my face and joy into my heart for the first time in weeks.

When the fun was over it was time to get down to serious business. Let me just paint the picture: a Scouser going to Old Trafford is never a particularly friendly occasion. A Scouser who had played for Everton can expect to suffer significant hostility. A Scouser who has been accused of child abuse, well I knew it wasn't going to be pretty.

I had known Sir Alex Ferguson for a few years, since the time I was manager of Stockport, as we were only based a few miles away from Old Trafford. I had the utmost respect for him as a person and for what he had achieved, especially in winning the treble of Champions League, FA Cup and Premier League the previous May. When we arrived at the ground, Sir Alex invited me into his room for a cup of tea.

"I'll be there in a few minutes, Sir Alex," I replied.

Having briefed my players about how we were going to approach the game, I made my way across the tight corridor that led to Sir Alex's room. We shook hands.

"You called me Sir Alex earlier, " he said.

"Yes I did." He had received his knighthood a short time previously. He looked at me embarrassed.

"Come on, David. You've known me long enough . . . " A brief pause. "Just call me 'Sir!'"

We burst out laughing. I talked with him about the accusations and how they had affected my family and I mentioned about how I would be going back to see the police the following week. To my astonishment, he said he wanted to walk out of the tunnel shoulder to shoulder with me. This was a magnificent gesture of support. He had made it clear he wanted to show the Manchester United faithful and the watching world that he was with me on this one. I felt he knew I was not capable of such evil behaviour.

As we walked out, the place erupted as it always does. At Old Trafford, as you emerge from the corner of the Stretford End stand you can see and hear the whole of that vast stadium. The noise was deafening as we made our way to the benches. I remember a United fan leaning towards me: "Best of luck Dave. You'll be fine."

Another United fan, with a shaved head, was next. He put his hand out. "Jones, we know you're innocent."

I wanted to stop in my tracks and walk straight over and shake his hand, but this was now work time and I kept my professional head on. Whenever you are at a ground where the walk to the bench is near to the crowd you can always hear abuse if it comes your way. To be fair I have never encountered that kind of behaviour at Old Trafford and there was none of it that day. In fact the response I got was wonderful and Sir Alex's gesture had played a big part.

The game itself was a cracker. Le Tiss scored twice and Marian Pahars got the other in a 3-3 draw. At the final whistle I walked over to Sir Alex for the customary handshake. He put his arm around my shoulder and whispered in my ear, "You can f****** well walk back to the dressing room on your own!" Classic Fergie.

CHARGED

THE FIRST TIME I actually met Stephen Pollard, the man who as my solicitor was going to become my lifeline over the next few months, was at Kingsley Napley's London offices. Ann came with me. The first thing Stephen said to me after we'd introduced ourselves was, "I'm going to ask you one question and depending on how you answer it will depend on whether I take the case. Did you do any of this?"

"No I didn't," I replied.

"Right," he said, "now let's start talking."

Stephen was a big wheel. He had represented all kinds of famous people. I daren't ask him what he was going to charge me, though at that point it was irrelevant to me anyway. All I wanted was to clear my name.

After a good hour's discussion, Stephen agreed to take the case and attend Wavertree Road police station with me for the pivotal meeting. As I drove up to Merseyside on Monday 27 September 1999 I was slightly apprehensive, but filled with renewed hope that Stephen would be able to put an end to the growing nightmare.

When we arrived, the same officers were there to greet me, but their mood had changed. Before, I had felt they were probing, and just making the kind of enquiries, asking the obvious questions, that they had to do in order to do their job properly. Now they were confident, verging on arrogant. Whereas last time they had been polite, now they were abrupt and abrasive. They had news for me – news they couldn't wait to break. The script I had hoped for was something like, 'Mr Jones the accusations have proved unfounded and are total lies. You are free to leave and we apologise for the hurt this has caused your family.'

Instead they looked me straight in the eyes. That second person from Clarence House who had made allegations of sexual abuse? They were now able to tell me what that accusation was – a word that shook me to the core. Buggery.

How I stayed on my feet I shall never know. Sexual abuse had been bad enough those few months earlier, but to be accused of buggery, the word slaughtered me.

"No, no, no, no, no," I heard myself shout. Falsely accuse me of anything, but please do not accuse me of doing that.

Someone had.

I then had to sit and listen to the repulsive details of what I was meant to have done. I will never be able to understand the sort of mentality that could invent such stories. I made another attempt to halt a situation that seemed to be spiralling out of control, but the officers did not seem to be interested in listening to what I had to say, behaving as if their minds were made up. At least that's how it seemed to me. It was as if they thought they were already talking to a convicted paedophile and I should sit there feeling full of guilt and shame.

Out came the words I had been dreading: "David Jones, we are charging you with . . ."

There were nine charges in all, each of them seemingly more depraved than the last.

I had to have my fingerprints taken and I was swabbed for the purposes of DNA. I might have imagined it, but as the female officer put the stick in my mouth to collect the sample she seemed to be judging me there and then. I felt physically sick. It was the lowest I have ever felt.

'Why me?' I kept thinking. I was so angry, even though Stephen tried to calm me down.

I remembered back to something Ann had said before I travelled up to Merseyside. She'd said that the police had been trawling and now they had caught a big fish. She firmly believed that once they had me in their sights they were going to work very hard to make something stick. I now understood that she was right.

Ann screamed as I phoned her to break the news I had been charged, calling those who had accused me "liars" and "bastards". When I rang off, her reaction cutting me to the quick, I stood for a moment inside the police station and felt this crushing weight bearing down on me and I thought the walls were closing in around me, stifling my breath.

The big fish, I realised, was caught in the net. Just as Ann had predicted.

Ann:

I had been getting more and more anxious, knowing that if they were going to release him without charge, they would have done it quickly. The longer it dragged on without hearing from Dave, the more negative I became.

When the phone rang, I rushed to it hoping beyond hope that our ordeal was going to end. I tried to work out what had happened from the first breath that Dave took before he spoke and from the sound of his voice. He was unbelievably calm as he told me what had happened. I was anything but.

Dave's coaching staff were in the house at the time, with their wives. They took the phone and talked to Dave who informed them of the news and then said he was on his way home.

Once I'd been left on my own, I kept thinking to myself that two of our co-workers from Clarence House had by now been sent to jail thanks to Operation Care. I just had this gut feeling that the police wanted to get more stripes on their arm in order to work their way up the ladder. Child abuse allegations were all the rage at that point in time and feathers in caps count for a lot more than you might think in the service. I had always feared that Dave would be charged and that we'd have a court case ahead of us. He was too big a fish to cast aside.

But I knew my husband. I knew he could not have done any of the things of which he was accused. He just was not capable of it. I had known Dave since he was 14. We were classic childhood sweethearts. He is a loving husband and father and our marriage is built upon trust. Our lives revolve around our children, we are completely family-orientated. Through childbirth, illnesses and accidents he was always there for me and the children.

There were other aspects to the case too, which seemed to have escaped the police's attention. I had worked with Dave at Clarence House and would surely have had some vague inkling of wrongdoing either on his part, or any other of our colleagues, but I had never heard or seen anything to suggest that abuse was going on. I had also been a registered child minder for ten years and Dave had always been around those children. We'd had to go through a lot of vetting procedures to reach that status and none of them had brought any issues to light.

When I had composed myself, my thoughts turned to how we would tell the children that their dad had been charged. We had already decided that if he was charged we would tell them the truth in as much detail as we could. Lea, Chloe and Danielle had to know everything so they could deal with what was in the papers and on the television. We knew it would begin to affect them and it wasn't long before Chloe came home from school saying kids had taunted her again about her dad being a paedophile.

When I told the two elder girls what had happened, they broke down and ran upstairs to their rooms. How do you handle that? It was a horrific situation.

Even our five-year-old Georgia was not immune. We had decided to protect her as much as we could from what was happening because we felt she was too young to understand, but she came home in tears one day when a boy at her school had said to her, "your daddy has been doing naughty things and he is going to prison."

We managed to gloss over that one and began to tell her little white lies, like when Dave returned home after being charged to find the press gathered outside the gates of our house for hours, she thought daddy had signed a new player who was really famous for the club. We didn't set her straight.

Now that Dave had been charged, our lives were in more turmoil than we had ever imagined. I had gone from being the wife of someone accused of being an abuser, to the wife of someone formally charged as a paedophile.

I knew nothing about courts and trials and I worried constantly that Dave could become a hostage to what assumptions people on the jury might make about him because of his profile and position. What would we do if enough of them didn't give a damn and just wanted their jury service over and done with, couldn't be bothered to think it all through and decided Dave was guilty because it was the easy thing for them to do? What if someone didn't like the look of him? Would the women on the jury think about it in a different way than the men?

I never told Dave this, but I used to lie awake at night visualising him going to prison and what might happen to him inside as a sex offender. Those thoughts persecuted me. I could not imagine taking the children to see him.

I knew Dave was innocent, but I worried constantly that he might end up as a martyr – the biggest sacrifice of all – so that Operation Care could be seen to be successful.

Dave:

I had always believed a man was innocent until proven guilty. You must be joking. That couldn't be further from the truth in my case.

"I am telling you now," I said as I left the station. "You are making the biggest mistake of your lives."

I was angry, distraught, shocked and frightened.

Outside the police station the street was teeming with press – a pack of wolves desperate to feed off a pack of lies. A few policemen were loitering by the station entrance eager, it seemed to me, to watch the show begin.

"Straighten yourself up, you've got to look good on TV," one of them said smugly. The chance of being afforded any dignity was beginning to look slim before the desk sergeant piped up, "Come over here, Mr. Jones, I'll get you out a different way."

And so he did. Still the press managed to scurry towards me, cameras flashing. Their questions hurled at me incoherently in all the chaos. In amongst the din I thought I could hear the words 'sexual abuse' as if they were being chanted.

The *Liverpool Echo* newspaper went to town in its edition that night. I often wonder if the reporters involved ever felt sorry about the way they handled my case since they reported it in the way that I felt the police saw it – I was already a guilty man as far as they were concerned.

I doubt they lost much sleep. Those who reported about the 'dark secret of the ex-Blues star' are hardly likely to get in touch with their conscience. But, although it may seem strange, I was angrier with the police than with the press. By charging me it seemed to me they were showing they believed these lies. As part of the charging process they had had to name my accusers for the first time and I learned that the pair who had come forward and were purveying these lies were a convicted armed robber and a transsexual arsonist. I was incredulous that they would be believed above me. It energised me to a huge extent. I was now ready to bang every door down and rattle every drum until people saw these accusations for what they were.

Ann:

I had lost any faith I had in the police and, a few months after Dave was charged, I decided I would agree to a press article where I could make the public aware of how our lives had become a living hell and how this intrusion had affected our children.

One of our friends who had been responsible for child protection at Clarence House was amazed that no-one from social services had yet been in touch with us. Accusers had claimed Dave was a child abuser, the police had charged him and yet we still had our own children living at our home. Obviously that showed us it was considered by the authorities that Dave was not a risk to his own children, which at least offered us some comfort. I made this point in the article: if we were such awful parents and my husband is such a monster, why haven't social services been near our doorstep?

Dave and I had talked about our fear that the children could be taken away from us. The very thought terrified us. As a wife and

Above and right, early signs of footballing prowess on holiday at Pontins in 1966. I was aged ten and in the team picture am in the front row, second from left. My elder brother Billy is back row, second from left.

In my early teens I joined Liverpool as Everton didn't seem to be interested in me. But as soon as I knew my idols wanted me I signed like a shot.

Proudly wearing the blue of Everton, my boyhood team.

Back in 1976, Mick Lyons and I both had Old English Sheepdogs. Mine was called Blue. Here we are with our dog groomer.

Everton team group 1976/77. I am in the second row, third from right.

In action for my new club club Coventry City. I moved to Highfield Road for £275,000 in 1979 when Everton manager Gordon Lee tried to turn me into a full-back, when I preferred to play centre-half. That was the beginning of the end for me at Goodison Park.

My best mate at Coventry was goalkeeper Les Sealey, whose antics were legendary. He got me into all sorts of bother.

Left, posing in the infamous 'Talbot' sponsored Coventry shirt. And right, with Gary Collier, my central defensive partner, signed from Bristol City at the same time as I arrived.

19 June 1976 – our wedding day; with my mum and dad.

Proud dad; with our first-born, Lea.

Having fun with Danielle (left) and Lea in Hong Kong.

With Georgia (left) and Chloe, my other two wonderful children.

In Hong Kong with Tommy Hutchison, who played for our rivals Bulova. Our coach is far left, while to my right is my Seiko team-mate Tim Bredbury.

Training with Seiko. Note the 'grass'.

Seiko FC 1981. I am in the second row, third from left.

Receiving the congratulations of Seiko owner CP Wong. We didn't lose a game while I was in Hong Kong, even though some of the local players used to wait until the second half to really turn it on so the boss would offer them bigger bonuses at half-time.

Winning trophies at non-league Mossley, where I was player-coach. The manager was Bryan Griffiths (centre) with the club physio on the left.

Danny Bergara gave me a job as youth team coach at Stockport County.

On the bench at Edgeley Park.

The Stockport squad from 1991/92, which reached Wembley twice in a week. Sadly we lost both finals, the Autoglass against Stoke and the play-offs against Peterborough. We also lost the Play-off final two years later against Burnley.

Taking Stockport into the big time: left, urging the team on from the sidelines as we push for a play-off spot in the Second Division in 1995/96; centre, smiling ruefully as we miss out on the last day of the season; right, Mike Flynn celebrates defeating Blackburn 1-0 in the League Cup in October 1996.

Defeating West Ham United at home in the League Cup quarter-final saw Stockport into their first ever semi-final as the wonderful 1996/97 season, which also saw us win promotion to the First Division, came to a climax.

After losing the home leg of the semi-final 2-0, no-one gave us a chance, but Sean Connelly's goal, left, put us within one goal of taking Premier League Middlesbrough to extra-time. Above, the Stockport fans go bananas as the goal goes in at the Riverside Stadium.

I became manager of Premier League Southampton in the summer of 1997. One of my first signings was goalkeeper Paul Jones, who I brought with me from Stockport. I would later take him to Wolves and he would become one of my best friends.

Our first brush with the law. On my first return to Goodison Park as a manager my coaches were reproached by a bobby – must've been something they said!

After finishing in 12th position in my first season in charge, 1998/99 was far tougher. We avoided relegation on the final day and celebrated amidst fantastic scenes. Above, I embrace midfielder Chris Marsden and, right, I acknowledge the fantastic Saints fans..

Left, walking out at the Dell for my first home game after being charged with those sickening offences. I was nervous about what to expect but the Southampton fans gave me a huge round of applause and remained supportive throughout my entire ordeal. I cannot thank everyone enough for showing faith in me during what was a terrible time in my life.

The irony of the police escorts which looked after me while their Merseyside Police colleagues hunted for 'evidence' to try to convict me of crimes I did not commit was not lost on me.

Watching my Southampton team succumb 5-0 to a rampant Newcastle. This would turn out to be my last away game in charge as Rupert Lowe put me on gardening leave shortly afterwards, bringing in Glenn Hoddle.

On my diving holiday in Thailand. I love diving, having taken lessons while I was manager of Southampton. It shocked me to discover that by going to Thailand whilst I was on gardening leave I was opening myself out to accusations and insinuations with people looking to justify the allegations against me simply because I'd gone on holiday.

A small selection of the thousands of cards which I received from from well-wishers and supporters and fellow professionals from clubs up and down the land which I received. I drew great strength from each and every one of these.

INSTANT CASH SCRATCHCARDS
Have you won today? PAGE 61

Can <u>any</u> woman ever be a good stepmum?

PAGES 34 & 35

GO CHRISTMAS SHOPPING TO FRANCE WITH P&O STENA FROM £1 PAGE 61

For 18 months, David Jones stood accused of paedophilia. Yesterday, in a damning indictment of the CPS and police, his ordeal ended

END OF THE NIGHTMARE

By **Andrew Loudon** and **Michael Seamark**

MAJOR questions hung over the way child abuse cases are investigated last night after the trial of soccer boss David Jones dramatically collapsed.

Crucial witnesses failed to turn up to face defence claims that they had invented their stories in the hope of winning compensation payouts.

After the Liverpool Crown Court judge discharged the jury, prosecutors accepted that it would be wrong to go for a retrial.

But their climbdown came too late to save the former Southampton manager and his family from 18 months of hell which cost him his £170,000-a-year job.

'It was just a nightmare,' he said as he hugged his wife Ann in delight and relief. 'Without the support of my family and friends, I would not have been able to get through this.'

The collapse of the trial

...ared at Liverpool Crown Court yesterday

...s 68-69, Coffee Break 70-72

Football manager cleared of sexual abuse

News

Premier League manager's abuse trial collapses
'You leave this court as an innocent man'

Former football manager cleared of child abuse charges

The collapse of the trial due to total lack of evidence was an incredible relief. It had seemed that the torture would never end, but thankfully it was all over in December 2000 and we could get on with our lives again.

Wolves offered me the opportunity to get back into management straight away and within two years we'd got together a side good enough to challenge for promotion.

All smiles as we beat Nottingham Forest in my first game in charge, left, and, above, I enjoy a joke on the bench. Getting back to doing what I love was a complete release after 18 months of hell.

Showing off the March 2002 Manager of the Month award for the First Division.

Wolves supporters were wonderful to me.

Returning to Southampton as Wolves manager was a very emotional moment for me and I was treated superbly by Saints fans once again.

Nathan Blake scores the second goal in our 3-0 victory over Sheffield United in the play-off final at the MIllennium Stadium in May 2003.

Left, showing off the Play-off final trophy at the Millennium Stadium after reaching the Premier League. Right, with Sir Jack Hayward as we parade the trophy around Wolverhampton and back to Molineux.

Enjoying a laugh in training with my assistant at Cardiff City, Terry Burton.

Celebrating winning the FA Cup semi-final against Barnsley, with Aaron Ramsey, now at Arsenal.

Leading my team out at Wembley for the FA Cup final was a dream come true. It was a fantastic day out for everyone from South Wales and I felt we played well, but lost to a better side on the day. But perhaps my proudest personal moment was being able to involve my grandsons Taylor, above right, and Luca, below right.

Embracing Portsmouth manager Harry Redknapp at the final whistle. It was disappointing to lose, but it was such a special time that it didn't crush us – far from it. We loved every minute.

Our Cup final celebration dinner; we threw a fantastic party just round the corner from Wembley and for once the losers probably had just as good a time as the winners!

And the party continued in superb style when we returned to Cardiff.

Chewing the cud with Cardiff City chairman Peter Ridsdale. Peter has had his ups and downs in football but I have found him to be a fntastic chairman to work for.

Under the spotlight at the start of the 2008/09 season which began with great expectations of us winning promotion to the Premier League.

Meeting Arsenal manager Arsène Wenger, the man to whom I sold Aaron Ramsey for £4.8m in June 2008.

With my Cardiff staff at a pre-match meal.

The 6-0 humiliation at Preston in April 2009 came as a total shock. Eventually it cost us dearly as we missed out on the play-offs to North End by just one, vital goal.

My frustration boils over as we lose 1-0 to Sheffield Wednesday and miss out on the play-offs at the end of the 2008/09 season. It was an utterly devastating experience and one I am determined to use to motivate the players to win promotion in 2009/10.

Visiting the magnificent new Cardiff City stadium in January 2009. The future of the club is incredibly bright. Moving in to the new training facilities and now the new ground will attract better players and move the club forward.

Above left, my daughter Georgia, Danielle's daughter Maddison and our lovely horse Roxy at our home just outside Cardiff. Above right, relaxing playing golf with journalist Bob Cass at the Vale of Glamorgan course.

Right, Ann and I enjoy our grand-daughter Maddison's christening

With Ann – the love of my life and number one supporter.

mother, the unbearable thought was that not only might I lose Dave, but that I could lose my children too. I wanted to tell the public that Dave was not seen to be a risk to his own family and that the allegations against him were lies.

A few days after the article was published in the Daily Mail, I collected the post one morning and amongst the letters was a brown envelope. I didn't need x-ray vision to work out what was inside. Surprise, surprise, Hampshire social services wanted to call round and 'have a chat'. The letter upset us both as the wording implied that we were both now under suspicion. Dave was furious and rang the contact number on the letterhead.

"I am not agreeing to social services visiting our house," he told them.

"It's just a matter of procedure, Mr. Jones. We just want to have a chat and make sure everything is alright."

"Everything's fine thanks. I don't want you in our house."

After the call we phoned our friend who worked in child protection and explained what was going on. We asked about the procedure. She explained that if social services arrived without a police officer then their interest would be more a matter of routine. But if a police officer arrived with them, then it was more serious.

Dave phoned social services back. "Do we have any choice about you coming to the house?"

There was a pause and I heard Dave say, "Will you be coming alone? Will you be the only person coming?"

The social worker said she would be, so, eager to show that there was absolutely no problem and no danger to our children we agreed to the visit. Like the police, social services have an important job to do. We both understand this. They have to investigate families. We were comforted it was only to be a routine visit.

Early the next morning the phone rang. After Dave had been charged I hated it when the phone rang. It was never good news. If you have ever had someone in your family seriously ill then you will know what I mean about feeling sick to the pit of your stomach when the phone rings. You develop a sixth sense. The ring tone is always the same, but somehow, and I don't know how, you can just tell who is ringing.

"That will be social services," I said.

Dave answered. I was right. They wanted to let us know that for some reason the ground had shifted overnight. They WOULD be bringing a police officer. A female police officer. "Why?" asked Dave.

"Procedure."

Dave was unequivocal. "That's not procedure. I know what this is about."

As soon as he put the phone down, I started to worry that everything could go horribly wrong.

Dave:

Children have to be protected and accusations have to be investigated. But I could not for the life of me understand the presumption of guilt against me – first the police, then social services and now it felt like every day I was on the front pages instead of being on the back pages, while every time I switched on the radio I heard the announcer say, "our top story, Southampton manager Dave Jones has been charged with sexual abuse." The way those stories were worded and, it seemed to me, delivered, assumed I was guilty. I could not escape.

On top of that a new dimension had been added to our nightmare as now merely the thought of what could happen to us was torturing us as much as the horrendous situation we were actually in.

I must be the only football manager in the world who can honestly say my job allowed me to keep my sanity. The evening after I was charged I drove back to Southampton to watch my reserve team play. That may seem odd given that I would soon be up at a Magistrates' Court to find out if the case was going to be sent trial, but I just wanted to try and shut the door on everything. Football would become my comfort zone.

Now, though, I was beginning to fear for what being charged would mean on that front too. I rang Stephen Pollard who agreed to come to our next home game and explain the procedure for what would happen from now on in to Rupert Lowe, which I was grateful for.

I felt there was a witch-hunt against me. But I also knew that to a certain extent I could choose whether to sink or swim. To me sinking was not an option. I had to find the courage to stand up for myself and, with the support of Ann and my family, and those close to me who believed in me, I strongly felt that I had to do it.

BACK TO WORK

WE SOON STARTED to get the feeling our phones were being tapped and our bins were being rummaged through. We had become very suspicious of everyone and everything. I can't prove it, but we learned that the police were leaving their calling cards with former Clarence House pupils saying should they remember something . . . anything, they should call.

Interesting, isn't it, how none of this took place while I was manager of lowly Stockport, before I became a Premiership manager? It just reinforced to me what Ann had said all along – they were out to net that 'big fish'.

It also seemed that every time I featured in a newspaper, another accusation would rise to the surface. The publicity was dredging up all sorts of scum ready to throw lies in my direction for the aforementioned 'compensation', all of whom were convicted criminals, most of them having never had a penny in their lives.

Amid all the frenzy – I was getting calls and messages of support from as far afield as Australia and Malaysia – I had a football team to run and thank goodness for that. Not that the timing was brilliant. I was charged on a Friday and Southampton didn't play again until the following Monday night. In my darkest moments I was now convinced there was a conspiracy against me and it even seemed like the televised games were deliberately planned against me. There were extra days for people to read all about the charges. And my first game would be in the full glare of Sky TV publicity.

As I drove to the ground I was extremely nervous about what was going to happen and what reaction I would receive. I really didn't know what to expect. As I drove into The Dell's car park I saw some stewards running towards the car. What on earth was going on? Was someone after me? They banged on the window. One of them shouted, "Keep going Dave. Don't give in."

Then a supporter shouted, "We are all with you Dave. We don't believe this crap." I was really grateful for the sentiment of all of them. There was no backlash, or at least no evidence of one.

Jim Smith was manager of our opponents that night, Derby County. He ran over to me – which, for Jim, is a feat in itself – gave me a huge hug and asked me how I was feeling. I told him I was looking forward to the game. It was an opportunity for him to talk about football, but Jim, unlike some other managers over the past few weeks, wanted to say what he thought about the charges.

"What a load of bollocks, Jonesy." Jim doesn't mince his words. "I can't believe they are saying all this stuff. It's a disgrace."

Without knowing what had happened at Old Trafford the previous weekend, he made a suggestion. "Listen, we'll walk out on the pitch together. You and me, Jonesy."

I was grateful for that too, but I explained to Jim that I really had to face this alone as it was my home crowd. In fact, for security reasons, there is always someone who walks out of the tunnel with you at Premier League games. At Southampton the big man who always walked out with me was a guy called Ralph. Ralph had his own way of showing his support for me. "If anyone says anything to you," he said, "I'll kill 'em."

Ralph was the sort of security guy who looked like he would bite the head off a live ferret for entertainment. I didn't think he was joking, but actually it was just the kind of levity I needed and I gave him a big smile.

At The Dell, players and staff called the walk from the dressing rooms to the pitch the 'walk of death'. It must be one of the longest walks in football. If you had performed badly it was torture. After giving my team talk, shaking the hands of every one of my players as they went out onto the pitch, as I always do, I started thinking, 'Oh God, I have got the walk of death now.' I had decided to do what I always do, and walk out on my own, just with Ralph alongside me. I set off, along the corridor, down some steps, up a walkway and then to the start of the tunnel. In normal circumstances that walk was long enough. That night it doubled in size.

I'm not one of those managers who shows emotion when I am out on the pitch. In the dressing room yes, but I always remain composed when I am on the touchline. Some supporters are critical of that. They want a manager who leaps about and performs to the gallery. I believe it is important for the manager to keep his passion under control when at the side of the pitch, not to let his emotions cloud his judgement. But that night I could not help but show emotion.

As I emerged into the floodlit stadium, the whole crowd stood up and applauded. I walked down the side of the pitch, and then looked up to see a mass of people. I welled up. That standing ovation meant so much to me and my family. Ann was in the stand and broke down in tears. I will never forget that moment, or those Derby fans in one corner of the ground who stood and clapped with their arms raised above their heads. It is a tradition in football that the away fans dish out as much stick as they can – but the Derby fans were joining in with the applause. Pure class.

The emotion seemed to communicate itself to the players. I don't believe they were consciously more motivated because of the situation, but they certainly started the match on a whirlwind. We were 3-1 up after an hour, moving the ball well and in complete control. I had been through one of the worst weekends of my whole life, but we were winning. This was manna from heaven for me.

Then somehow Derby clawed their way back to 3-3, scoring an equaliser in the last minute. Talk about going through every possible emotion: the build-up to the game, walking out and the match itself. But it was the reaction of our supporters which gave me so much strength.

During the post-match interviews I was told that Sky TV commentator Alan Parry had been ticked off by one of his bosses. He had got caught up in all the emotion himself and had asked viewers on air how anyone could believe that I could commit such crimes.

I BEGAN TO receive letters of support from all over the country. Even some that simply said 'Dave Jones, Southampton manager, United Kingdom' on the envelope found their way to me.

Not all opposing fans were that supportive or benign, however. Our next home game was against Liverpool. I had hoped that the travelling Scousers would show support for one of their own. As it happened one of the things that hurt me most was the reaction of a minority of Liverpool fans. I stress it was a minority. Okay, so I am a Blue nose, but above all I'm a Scouser. A section of the Liverpool fans chanted the most disgusting abuse in my direction. My family were in the stands having to listen to it and after the game both Gerard Houllier and Phil Thompson, the Liverpool management team, sought me out to apologise on behalf of the club. So did the Liverpool chairman and amongst the subsequent letters I received from Liverpool supporters was one from a female fan who said she left the ground at half-time because she couldn't bear the chanting.

I'm a Liverpool lad and when times are tough we should all stick together, but a section of Liverpool fans stuck a knife in me that day – in stark contrast to how Everton supporters treated me earlier in the season after the initial accusations. Right from the moment I got off the team bus at Goodison there was nothing but whole-hearted support. It helped ease some of the pain.

Sadly the FA saw fit to intervene, even though at this stage I was still the full-time manager of a Premier League club. Each year, when the YTS boys were signing their first contracts, they used to come to our house and we'd meet and greet the families. Ann would prepare some food to make them all feel at home as they took their first steps in the game. Suddenly, without any warning, the FA's compliance officer, Graham Bean, put a stop to it. Just like that. I phoned him up absolutely furious and asked him what on earth he thought he was doing. He told me he couldn't risk the children being in my house. It wasn't right, he said, for them to be seen there. I ask you, how callous can you get? He had no evidence, nothing, just hearsay and allegations to go on. His organisation, the FA, were the only organisation in the whole of the football world who treated me this way.

YOU'VE JUST KILLED

MY HUSBAND

THE SOUTHAMPTON SUPPORTERS treated me superbly throughout this initial, very difficult, period and I tried my best to repay them by concentrating on the job I was doing for the remainder of the season. People told me that they were astonished at how I seemed outwardly to be coping. Luckily I do have this ability to compartmentalise things and just get on with it.

In January 2000 my court date came through. It was set for November, in ten months' time. After weeks of few developments, it seemed to be the straw that broke the camel's back as far as Southampton Football Club were concerned.

The chairman Rupert Lowe had always been very big on bonding amongst his staff and used to organise things for us like going shooting or to a spa. We had just been heavily beaten by Newcastle 5-0 at St. James' Park and to try and engender some team spirit we were all out go-karting when Rupert rang me out of the blue and told me he'd like to see me that evening. I could tell from his voice that something was not quite right. He was normally very chatty, but this time he was cagey, almost distant. As soon as Rupert said he'd like to see me, I got an inkling as to why that was. Wondering if I was being over-sensitive, I acted on my instinct by saying, "If you're going to get rid of me, let's do it at the office, not at my house."

He replied that this wasn't the case, he simply had some good news and some bad news. He just wanted to discuss "a few things".

The day before I had filled Rupert in – as I kept doing – about the latest meeting with my solicitor. He was always interested and appreciative of the updates, but on this particular occasion he had had to rush off. He said he was having someone to dinner, though he never told me who his guest was. Later, I discovered it was Glenn Hoddle, my nemesis, the man who ended up following me from club to club.

I called Ann and told her Rupert was coming to the house. Immediately she said it was because he was going to sack me. Me, being me, I tried to play it down – after all, there was good news as well as bad wasn't there? And he had said he was not going to sack me.

That evening, Rupert duly arrived, accompanied by Managing Director Andrew Cowen. Ann gave them both a kiss, went into the kitchen to make a cup of tea and was gone for no more than a minute when the shit hit the fan. Rupert quickly told me they were putting me on gardening leave to allow me to concentrate on fighting my case and were going to appoint former England coach Glenn Hoddle as temporary manager.

I told him, "You don't need to do that. And if you're going to appoint Glenn Hoddle, just let me leave totally."

He said that was out of the question since they eventually wanted me to come back.

"No Rupert," I replied, "if you do this, I'll never come back."

Just as I said that, Ann walked back into the lounge with the tray of drinks.

"Go on Rupert. Tell her," I said. He couldn't, but then he didn't need to, his silence spoke a thousand words.

In her anger, Ann knocked the tea over and uttered the immortal line, "You've just killed my husband. You've just stabbed him in the back."

THE GOOD NEWS, it turned out, was simply that Rupert and the club wanted me back after the trial was concluded successfully.

Ann asked whether, if that was the case, the club could put in writing that Glenn Hoddle would then step aside, but Rupert hedged his bets and said that could only be discussed nearer the time. All this while I was sitting in stony silence, seething with rage. I had no desire to continue working for someone who treated me like this. How could I? The trust had gone.

"Pay me up," I demanded, "and let me go."

He refused, maintaining that the club would carry on paying me and that I should go away on a little holiday and that I could still go scouting for them since Glenn's forte wasn't really finding players. The more he spoke, the further I felt the dagger being pushed in.

"You want me to find players for someone you are putting in my job?" I asked. "Let him go and find his own players."

Ann's anger boiled over and she asked them to leave the house. From my standpoint, I understood the team wasn't doing as well as Rupert may have wished, but in that case they should have just paid me off. Rupert tried to make out that he was giving me gardening leave so I could concentrate on the court case, but I couldn't have told him more clearly that there was nothing I could do. It was progressing perfectly well. I was going to London every six weeks or so, but there was nothing else that could really be done until I went to court the following November.

I have to ask myself if there might have another motive for Rupert asking me to step aside. Perhaps he felt he couldn't have a manager at a Premiership club on abuse charges. So why didn't he just sack me? I guess he was scared of the furore that would have ensued. He'd have been crucified by the press. It would have looked as though I was guilty in the club's eyes, wouldn't it?

One other thing may have influenced Rupert's decision to dispense with my services. The club had just signed up new sponsors, Friends Provident, a finance company who pride themselves on ethics. Maybe he didn't want their boat to be rocked by the potential scandal he would have on his hands if I was found guilty. Southampton were a couple of seasons away from moving into their new stadium and I think the chairman was worried in case I actually ended up being convicted and his continued support for me cost him the deal.

I can understand why he might feel like that purely from a business point of view, yet I couldn't quite understand why, after supporting me for the first half of the 1999/2000 season, he suddenly backed off. Certainly I had not been doing my job any differently. Ask any of the players and they will tell you that, had it not been for what they read in the papers, none of them would have ever known what was going on.

I was now very angry – mostly because this was yet another hammer blow to me on top of everything else that was going on.

Anyway, Rupert told me he wanted to hold a press conference the following day, with me sitting one side of him and Hoddle on the other, to tell the football world why the changes were being made. Insensitive or naïve, or a bit of both? For me it was a total non-starter and that was the moment when my patience finally snapped and I told him to "f*** off and get out of my house."

PREMIER LEAGUE TO GARDENING LEAVE

THE EVENING OF Rupert Lowe's bombshell, I summoned all the coaching staff to the house to tell them the news. I remember the reaction of Stuart Gray, my assistant. "Does that mean I'm just going to be the bibs and ball man now?" he asked. He knew how dictatorial Hoddle was and also that Glenn was bound to bring in his own men, leaving most of my staff out in the cold.

After I'd turned down his idea of the press conference, Rupert had told me he didn't want me to go into the club the next day, but I wanted to say goodbye to the players. He then said he'd be there too, but I didn't want him to be. I went in and saw the players on my own – and told them the reasons why I was leaving. Every one of them was incredibly supportive and, if truth be told, somewhat annoyed with the board.

Later that day Rupert was holding the press conference to introduce Glenn Hoddle. He was still adamant that I was going to come back even though he had appointed Hoddle in my place. I'd already told him I would never accept that. I had my pride. I asked my secretary Daphne, who was distraught at the turn of events, to clear my desk and then sneaked out the back to avoid hundreds of press.

When I got home all my staff and their families were at my house once again. It was a wonderful gesture for them to all gather together and there were a lot of tears. That meant a lot to me. Conversely, what really annoyed me was that Hoddle never even had the decency to phone me. He got his assistant John Gorman to do it. I thanked John for the call, but told him he shouldn't have been the one making it. It wasn't him who had taken my job.

Southampton suspended me on full pay while Hoddle took over, which Rupert still believes was perfectly reasonable. I knew there could be no way back for me at the club, though. All I wanted to do was to sever my links with them and be allowed to move on. I took my case to the LMA Managers' Arbitration Tribunal to be released from my contract so I could look for another job. Much to my frustration, the panel ruled in favour of the club, as their lawyer came up with a precedent-setting case which had fallen in favour of the employer. Not long after the tribunal we came to a compromise agreement and, although I am not at liberty to give any details, it certainly did not involve the remainder of my contract being fully paid up, plus I gave up certain bonuses. But the main thing was that I was happy to get out of it all.

It may sound odd, but I do still quite like Rupert Lowe. It's just that I felt he let me down. I felt I was being made a scapegoat by the football club, but friendship is friendship, business is business. I had a really good working relationship with him over the years. True, picking players was not his greatest strength – after all that is the duty of the manager. To give you an example of this, although admittedly it is one that Rupert himself tells me he does not recall, we were abroad together watching a game containing a potential target and midway through the first half Rupert piped up by saying something like, "Oh I don't like him, he doesn't seem very good." It turned out that he was watching a different team and a different player to the one I had travelled to run the rule over.

But let's get one thing absolutely straight. Rupert's biggest achievement remains relocating Southampton FC from its cramped home at The Dell, which held only 15,000 of those wonderful fans, to St Mary's – which houses twice as many. His other legacy is an academy that has produced fine players such as Gareth Bale and Theo Walcott. He may have been a controversial figure for Saints fans over the years, but to me these achievements speak volumes about the direction he was attempting to take the club when relegation intervened, bringing a whole new set of problems which, by that time, were nothing to do with me.

LUCKILY I HAVE a lot of friends in football. Alan Curbishley, who was then manager of Charlton, invited me to help at training within days of me leaving Southampton; Gary Johnson also called me up. Gary was manager of Latvia at the time. He asked me to go and scout for him, which was a massive boost. It got me out of the house and I was travelling, feeling involved again. Other managers also got in touch with me to do similar tasks and it kept my hand in ready for when I returned full-time.

One of the first things I did, within a week or so of leaving Southampton, was to go on a break scuba diving in Thailand – but not before I got a call off my uncle. He was an ex-bobby and asked me whether I thought it was a wise move going on holiday to Thailand. I couldn't, for the life of me, see what he was getting at until he told me about the connotations of that country. It is, after all, the destination of choice for convicted paedophiles and is renowned for cross-dressing 'ladyboys'. I just hadn't considered what could be read into me going for a break somewhere like that. What hit me hardest was that I could go off and do something so utterly innocent like this and it could potentially rebound on me extremely badly – headlines, gossip and, worse, conclusions being leapt to by the police.

To be honest, I was quite angry. I wasn't going to let anyone stop me doing what I wanted to do, no matter what might be construed from it. I asked Ann what she thought and she was of the same opinion as me – keep things as normal as possible and try not to let people, despite all the innuendo, affect our lives. So I went to Thailand with a friend, and his mate, and had a fantastic time.

We went diving in the morning, then back to the hotel, then night-diving. I was doing something I really loved as I had done all the courses around Southampton over the previous few years for relaxation. Yet I could never totally escape being recognised. I was lounging around by the pool one day and I got this feeling that this woman was taking pictures of me. It happens all the time as a manager when you are on holiday and I'm not normally remotely bothered by it, but this was different. Wherever I went, this woman seemed to be there. Then I got a phone call from a friend of mine – a journalist who I won't name – who told me that he knew there had been reporters engaged to follow me, while I was in Thailand. My skin crawled.

When I returned, I played as much golf as possible and went to the gym every day. It was important for me to stay fit and it kept me focussed and sharp mentally. In the early stages I had just lounged around at home and that just wasn't me. I remember Ann saying to me "healthy body, healthy mind" and from that day on, I kept myself in shape.

I hate the phrase 'gardening leave' more than I hate the thought of gardening itself. I had been in football, either as a player or manager, for the best part of 25 years. Now I had every second of every day to think about the mess that I was in, with nothing positive to hold onto on a daily basis. With the trial still eight months away I missed the day-to-day involvement dreadfully.

Ann and I went on a couple of holidays together and still used to have the Southampton staff and players round to the house, people like Paul Jones and Chris Marsden, both of whom I'd previously managed at Stockport. It was great to still have that contact and also for those lads to show that they believed in me still. They were top pros as well as superb people and I really appreciated their regular shows of support.

THE TIME MY lack of involvement in football really hit me was when the following 2000/01 season kicked off. The start of the season normally falls on or around my birthday, August 17th, and Ann had arranged for us to go paint-balling as a birthday present. She knew I'd feel awful not being involved in football so arranged something to occupy the day. All our friends and family came, but I was so wound up I killed half my own team as well as the opposition. Anyone in my way just got fired at. All I could think of was that I was running around a field firing coloured pellets when I should have been on the touchline at Derby's new Pride Park stadium managing my Southampton team.

By now, we had moved into a world I had never previously experienced. We'd hired a private detective because I wanted to find out as much as I could about the people who were accusing me. When you go to a solicitor in a scenario like this, you want them to say, 'We've got all the information about what the prosecution have on you so don't worry, everything's going to be alright'. But that's not how it works. Everything is kept under wraps. That's why we engaged the private investigator. He had already done some work for the Premier League and I later found out he had also worked for Peter Ridsdale, my Cardiff City chairman, when Peter was at Leeds.

The investigator discovered that one of my accusers had given evidence to the police claimng that I had once driven him to Morecambe on his own and abused him in this mythical red car the police were so interested in. This was totally untrue.

Another accuser had stated that I used to deliberately take my son Lea into work on a Saturday morning because I knew that he fancied Lea. Words fail me. Lea was nine or ten at the time and this person said in his statement that on one occasion he kissed Lea on the lips. It sickens me to think about that. Can you imagine, when we told our Lea, now 25 years old, what the guy had said, what his reaction was? He was hopping mad to put it mildly. It irked me that the police never once bothered to ask Lea himself about the accusations.

I don't know how much we paid the private investigator to find out what he could, but it must have been in excess of £20,000. That, however, paled into insignificance compared to what the whole case would eventually cost us. I have never talked about this before but between being suspended and being acquitted it cost us at least £400,000. We were running very short of money and had to put our house up as collateral after the solicitors asked for guarantees that I would pay. Okay I was suspended on full pay, but almost all of that money was spent clearing my name. Fans assume people like me are loaded, but my managerial career had only really taken off 18 months earlier. Yes I was earning good money at Saints, but everything we'd saved was now being swallowed up on legal costs and the private investigator.

We tried to behave as normally as we could despite the fact that funds were being drained and we forced ourselves to take a number of holidays, shortish breaks, to alleviate the pressure on us as a family. One trip in particular sticks in my mind. Because of the press and everything else that had invaded our lives, we decided we'd visit Mauritius. On the way out we were standing in the airport surrounded by all these well-to-do people in their straw hats and I felt completely anonymous for the first time in months. No-one knew who I was. I liked it that way.

When we landed we were picked up by private taxi and, before we got in the car, Ann asked how much the local currency was to the pound. Based on that I gave the driver what I thought was a reasonable amount and he seemed chuffed to bits. When we arrived at the hotel, everyone ran at me to help me out, doing this for me, that for me, pampering me and Ann like there was no tomorrow. Even when the hotel's straw roof caught fire no-one seemed to take any notice. It was only when we got into the bedroom that I realised why. The local currency was 38 to the pound, not 380, which is what I thought I had heard our driver say. Word must obviously have spread like wildfire that I was the most generous guy on the planet! I probably gave that taxi driver about a week's wages for that one ride.

I smiled to myself and, as we got inside the room and put down the bags and turned on the TV, the live game on Sky was . . . Southampton against Arsenal. In many ways it was the last thing I wanted to see, but I still loved the place and the people. Still do, in fact. To see what has happened to the club in the last few years, with it being relegated to the third tier of English football and coming so close to oblivion in the spring of 2009, saddens me deeply.

About a month before we were due to go to court, I went with my brother Mark, his brother-in-law Jeff, who was a policeman, and a friend of theirs, a solicitor called Ian, to Portugal on a golfing trip. Unbeknown to me, the policeman and the solicitor had planned while we were away to sit me down and prepare me for how to deal with my forthcoming ordeal. They told me I should answer questions with a straight yes or a no and not go into some long explanation to justify my actions. It helped focus me on the specifics of what was about to happen and I really appreciated their advice.

Although I had not anticipated this kind of conversation, I quite enjoyed the holiday – we played a lot of golf and it really did help me get my mind in gear for the trial. When I returned from Portugal, I learned – again through the private investigator – that some of the prisoners who knew my accusers but who had nothing to do with my case were actually getting angry about it inside various jails. They were behind bars but even they seemed to know my case was a scam.

Those breaks we took stood me in good stead as I prepared myself mentally for the arduous task ahead – proving myself innocent when so many seemed to have already written me off.

PARANOIA AND THE
SOCIAL SERVICES

I WAS NOW certain that I was being stitched up either by the police or, in my darker moments, by a newspaper. There was no other way of making any sense of it all. Ann was convinced the house was bugged. There were times we would talk on the phone and hear clicking noises, typical of those which you hear in the movies when that kind of thing is going on. I am still convinced today that this was the case, but we can't prove it, or who was behind it.

In any event the fear it induced in us manifested itself in numerous ways, some of which seem ridiculous now looking back. The thing is that when you are going through such a hideous experience it is very difficult to keep a perspective, to retain a sense of who you are. I tried to keep a sense of perspective, but Ann, in short, was becoming paranoid.

Ann:
You may think I'm exaggerating when I use the word paranoia, but that's what I had begun to feel. When your husband has been charged with sexually abusing children you become paranoid about the way people look at you, about what they are talking about out of earshot, about what they might read into your every movement. A meaningless

glance brings untold dark thoughts surging to the forefront of your mind and you begin to speculate wildly why a person in a supermarket might do a double-take or look at you for that extra fraction of a second. They could simply be scanning the shelves for bargains, but that was not what was flashing through my mind each and every time someone glanced my way.

I am convinced our phones were being tapped, so much so that sometimes I would drive two miles to use a phone box to phone my sister just so that I could have a private conversation without anyone listening in.

I remember one sunny August morning when Dave was teaching Georgia, who was then five years old, how to ride a bike. I looked out into the garden and couldn't believe what I saw. She was dressed in layers of clothing as if it was mid-winter. She had pads on her elbows, shins and knees, her cycling helmet covered her head and she sweated buckets as she pushed the pedals round.

"What are you doing, Dave?" I asked.

In actual fact I knew exactly what he was doing. He did not want his daughter to get any marks on her body if she fell off her bike in case they were misconstrued and came back to haunt us in any way. He turned to me.

"You're right. What the hell am I doing?"

It was one little incident which exemplifies exactly what we felt every minute of every day. I even became frightened to bath Georgia. I used to give her the flannel to wash herself because I dare not touch her.

One evening she said to me, "Mummy, my wee wee is sore."

I could see that she probably had a urine infection, but I was too frightened to take her to the doctor in case he reported to the authorities that my daughter was sore in a private area. That's how bad it had got for me.

Inevitably, following that article I had written in a national newspaper, the day came when Social Services arrived. We had told them they were not welcome, but once they had arrived we made them so just the same. It was such an invasion having them in our home. I wanted to scream, 'Get out of my house, get away from my family.'

They were not aware of it, but we had become so concerned about Dave being misrepresented that we secretly taped their interview with us just *in case it was not reported with word-for-word accuracy. We hid a tape recorder behind a vase in a room.*

They asked us if the children were happy, if we had any problems, and other general questions. Then they said they wanted to interview our two youngest, Georgia and 14-year-old Chloe. We refused.

They were adamant they wanted to interview Georgia. They told us they had the power to go into schools and interview children away from the family home if they wanted to. That obviously didn't go down too well with us. We felt threatened by that very suggestion. They were quite clearly saying, 'if you don't give permission, we will do it anyway.'

Dave was polite but blunt. "If you have to interview my children you can interview the two eldest, Lea and Danielle. They were children we'd had when I was meant to have carried out this abuse in Clarence House. Chloe and Georgia were not even born then."

We had absolutely no problem about the older children. In fact we wanted them to be interviewed. The authorities eventually wrote to Danielle, who was 17, stating that if she wanted to speak to them privately away from the house then they could arrange that. Danielle wrote back saying there was 'no reason on earth' why they should not interview her in her own home. Dave was not allowed to be in the house when they did so. I guess that was 'procedure' too. He was unhappy about this but reluctantly agreed.

When they returned to conduct the interview with Danielle, I thought it reasonable to at least offer them a cup of tea. They refused. They were here for one reason, and one reason alone. Danielle was in the lounge and I must have followed a mere three minutes later. As I walked in, they walked out. Interview over. "Do you honestly think I would still be living in this house, at my age, if my father was a paedophile?" Danielle had told them. That put them in their place.

The next interview was with Lea. I couldn't be there so our close friend Joanne O'Neil – who had been a child protection officer who Dave had worked with at Clarence House – went to Lea's house instead. Lea was so angry about what was happening to his dad. He was also furious that one of the accusers had included Lea in his statement; the same guy who, as Dave has already mentioned, claimed Dave knew he was attracted to

Lea. I told Lea that when people are telling lies they can't remember details, so not to worry. They always trip themselves up in the end. I did firmly believe that, but when I said it to him it was also a bit of bravado to give Lea confidence to stand up for what he believed in – his father.

We were worried, though, that Social Services might provoke Lea during the interview by using some of the more gruesome details of the allegations. Our son can be volatile when he feels unfairly treated or wronged. As it happens, they did ask him about that allegation, but he kept his cool enough to make his point that as far as he was concerned it was a load of nonsense.

That was another short interview with one of our children. The evidence had shown there was nothing to investigate. Social Services didn't even have the courtesy to let us see their final reports. They never even put in writing to us that in their view our children had never been at risk and would never be. That must have been their professional judgement because we never heard from them again.

Dave:

To me that spoke volumes. The workers from Social Services had obviously come into the situation thinking that I was guilty and they would find a household full of children who had suffered years of sickening abuse which they would be desperate to tell them about in order to escape their living hell. Instead they were sent away with a flea in their ear, clearly drawing the swift conclusion that there was absolutely no foundation to any fears that our children were being abused.

These people have a job to do, I realise that, but to be on the receiving end just makes you feel so dirty.

As Ann says, Social Services did not communicate their findings to us or the police. They just melted away. At least we had dealt with that threat to our family. Plenty of others lay ahead.

NAILED TO THE
FLOORBOARDS

THE MORE THINGS that were getting thrown at me, the more angry I was becoming. I was annoyed that I was paying taxes to keep these people who were accusing me in prison, taxes to pay for the police who were crucifying me and huge bills to my solicitor who was defending me. Everywhere I looked, I was frittering money away – money I had saved for my family and my children – on defending these lies that had been chucked at me.

With my trial looming, I had come to terms with the fact that I had to prepare as well as I could for what might happen if I lost. I spent a lot of time in the weeks leading up to the case getting my house in order and making sure that if everything went wrong for whatever reason, Ann would be okay to meet the mortgage payments and be able to look after the kids. I didn't tell her what I was doing because I knew she would have gone ballistic. If you drew a chart of 1 to 100 how confident I was of the whole thing being thrown out, it was a 99. But it was that one per cent I was concerned about. I'm quite methodical in what I do. When I go to away matches, I make sure everything is ready well in advance – my clothes, my suit, my tie, my socks. I work backwards to make sure I have everything. It's the same at the games themselves. Maybe because of the impression I give of being laid back, people often think I've missed something on the pitch when in fact I haven't missed a trick. It is the same in my personal life: I needed to ensure that everything would be okay for Ann if it had all gone pear-shaped. I knew, though I never told the family, that if I had been convicted there was no way I would have allowed her or the kids to come and see me inside. I know how much that would have upset her, but I would just have felt too embarrassed and degraded. These were the kind of thoughts going through my head as November 2000 approached.

In August, three months before the trial, worried about the fact I felt I had to prove my innocence, rather than the other way around, I took a gamble. On the recommendation of Jeff, my brother Mark's brother-in-law, I booked an appointment with Ray Wyre, one of the country's top forensic psychiatrists. Jeff had been to seminars with Ray and had heard a lot about his work on historic abuse of children. He suggested I should go and see Ray in order to re-assure myself.

When we arrived, Ann waited outside. I sat down with Ray in his room and he warned me that he was recording the session and that if he discovered any paedophile tendencies, he would be obliged to report his findings. I was perfectly happy with this, so Ray began his examination. After about ten minutes of questioning, much of it personal stuff, he halted the interview.

"You're f***** useless," he told me.

"What d'you mean?" I asked, surprised and not understanding what he was getting at.

"I ask you what your fantasies are and you tell me you dream about a big house in Florida, winning the FA Cup or being manager of England . . . I'm talking about sexual fantasies!"

I honestly didn't realise that was what he had meant, but his description of me as "f***** useless" for some reason lifted a huge weight off my shoulders. Ann said I looked a different person after that. I felt that if we had someone as well-respected as Ray Wyre stating his opinion that I had no tendencies towards paedophilia at all then I was beginning to have a fantastic case. Ray even offered to be an expert witness for me.

Ann:

The Ray Wyre session certainly helped Dave and it was very necessary for us to have a lift at that point. For the first time in 25 years we were on top of each other every minute of every day. I went through some dreadful mind games. I'd be wiping the floor and at the same time have visions of driving to Winchester prison and seeing Dave looking dishevelled slumped behind a desk. I was becoming more and more mechanical in doing every day things and more and more distracted. On one occasion, I came out of the supermarket with £90-worth of shopping I had forgotten to pay for. Suddenly I saw a security guy with a walkie-talkie. He wasn't talking about me, but it made me realise what I'd done and I scooped everything back from the car boot into the trolley and rushed off to pay. That was the sort of effect everything was having on me.

There were other examples of paranoia. I became frightened even of taking Georgia to the doctor in case some outrageous new suggestion of abuse was made against us because of some bump she'd picked up doing PE at school or playing in the playground. I had never had these worries and feelings before, but as the trial approached, seemingly slower and slower as we inched ever closer to it, this was how the situation twisted its vice-like grip on us.

Dave:

Our private investigator had uncovered more evidence of the police's 'trawling' of prisons, which had led to these accusations being made about me.

'Trawling' is the name the police themselves give to the process of asking questions of prisoners about their youth and who abused them, waiting to see who they can catch in their nets, not giving two hoots about what would happen to innocent people like me who are snared. But how on earth did prison inmates end up coming forward with these lies in such disgusting graphic detail? I'll tell you how: because they knew there was money in it for them if their stories sounded convincing. If you've been in prison most of your adult life, wouldn't you be tempted? Wouldn't you do almost anything to improve your lot?

I was identified by police and their 'snouts', as they are called in the trade, as someone who had been an abuser. It happened, I firmly believe, because I was by now a reasonably high profile person, being a Premier League manager. I feel sure I was targeted and that the police were out to snare me as I would be a newsworthy catch. In that sense they had been proved very right – the papers were hounding us every single day – they were just so wrong about me having ever been an abuser. I always felt, at every stage of the investigation, that my status was more important to them than any proof of my guilt.

Ann's sister Linda, who we haven't talked much about but who was so supportive throughout, wrote to Home Secretary Jack Straw saying how disgusted she was with the police's use of trawling to gather evidence. She told him that it's an iniquitous way of operating – to go looking for a crime to see if anyone remembers anything untoward, based on offering inducements. It was a practice that had started in the United States, but they soon realised it didn't work, that all it was doing was making the judicial system an absolute farce, creating a compensation culture. As it turned out Jack Straw didn't have a clue what Linda was talking about. We saw the pro forma letter that came back saying, with classic official standoffishness, that we had to let the judicial system run its course. Typical.

This appalling 'investigative technique' had already seen others convicted on flimsy evidence simply because it is almost impossible to prove that you haven't done something. Society is conditioned to believe the abused rather than the accused in these emotional and distressing cases. The situation is loaded against the defendant. And here I was caught in that trap. I felt like I was being nailed to the floor-boards.

ON TRIAL

I HAD BEEN determined, throughout my so-called sabbatical, not to turn into a vegetable. I'd been told about how innocent defendants who lost their jobs were nervous wrecks by the time they got to court. That wasn't going to happen to me if I could possibly help it. From the very first day after the charges, I tried to keep myself busy. I got the power hose out, painted the garage, things like that. Mundane perhaps, but important to my sanity.

We were determined to preserve a sense of normality. A party we had been planning for a year duly went ahead with over 100 guests, including a good number of Southampton players and their families. It was vital for me to keep my dignity and it helped that none of our friends believed the allegations. Georgia's circle of friends continued to come and stay the night – none of their parents were remotely worried about the case – but being without football, both on match days and training, was killing me. It was as if someone had pressed pause and put my life on hold. I couldn't wait to get back in the game on a full-time basis.

The closer we got to the trial, the harder it became to sleep properly. Ann and I tended to stay awake discussing what might or might not happen until the wee hours. Ann was becoming increasingly agitated and restless even though there was so much support for me in and around Southampton. People would come up to me and say, "Keep your chin up, Dave." Many of these people didn't know me at all. It meant the world to me.

It seemed as if only my accusers and the prosecuting team were against me. It took us a couple of months to realise that every time I was picking the phone up to call my solicitor, I was getting charged. But I was permanently inquisitive about how the legal side was proceeding. We had decided to try to discredit the witnesses who were making up these lies about me, so the private investigator was called into action again. The more I learned about these people it just brought home to me the desperate plight they themselves were in. Jailed for long periods, with little hope. No prospect of anything approaching what we might call a normal life. What did it matter to them whether they won the case or not? It was a nice little earner either way and they had nothing to lose. Unlike me.

And then the day arrived: time to leave for the make or break trial at Liverpool Crown Court. Ann was dreading leaving the house, while I was in one of my quiet moods. I wasn't whistling either. I'd better explain that comment. Whenever I go away on a trip – any trip – I tend to whistle as I prepare everything and it really bugs Ann. I guess she must think it means I'm happy to be leaving! In all seriousness, when I go quiet it's my thinking mode kicking in. My PA at Cardiff will tell you that me being silent worries her because it means I'm thinking something up or I'm ready to go and do battle with someone.

I felt very prepared for what was about to happen as I'd been over and over everything with my legal team. We believed we were going to get a result. But I was utterly unprepared for the traumatic farewell we faced. Ann's sister, Dot, had come down to look after the girls, take them to school and try to keep things as normal as possible. As I kissed them all goodbye, they were very quiet. I quickly discovered why. They were just holding back. The older ones knew what was going on, though little Georgia thought we were just going away for a couple of nights.

Just before we left, our 16-year-old, Chloe, handed Ann a card she had made especially for me, telling me how much she loved me and how hurt she was by what was happening. Ann thought I would be too distressed to read it, so she kept it hidden until we were in the car. It made for tearful reading. Chloe didn't often express her feelings, but in the card she poured her heart out.

> *Dad,*
> *I never say this to your face, so I'm telling you on paper how much I love you. I'm not the world's most perfect child and I'm at an age where I never show affection towards my parents, but you mean the world to me. I want to take away your pain, but I can't.*
>
> *The people accusing you are nothing and you are every-thing. Stand up to them, Dad, and show them you are strong. They will never break you.*
>
> *I don't believe in God because I don't see how he can allow these things to happen to such a good man. But I do believe in hope and faith, and most of all I believe in YOU.*
> *Love Chloe XXX*

We later learnt from Dot that no sooner had we left the house than the two eldest girls just broke down in the hall, collapsing in a sobbing heap. Dot tried everything she knew to keep their spirits up, but they were inconsolable. The reality of what could happen had hit them, hard.

About 20 minutes after we left, Mr and Mrs Gordon – directors of Southampton FC who lived on the same road as us – came round with flowers and a good luck card. They didn't realise we'd already gone, but it was such a generous touch.

I must say I'm so proud of the girls and Lea. I can only imagine what they had to go through. In fact, I warned Lea not to get involved if anyone said anything nasty about me to him during the trial period. "Just smile and nod your head," I told him, because he would have found it easy to fly off the hook. He's that kind of a guy, Lea: fiercely loyal to his family.

The drive up to Liverpool was a pretty silent affair except for us discussing Chloe's card. I said to Ann that a child of that age should not have to write such emotional things. Voicing that opinion made both of us think back over everything we'd been through in the past 18 months.

Ann and I had booked into the Crowne Plaza hotel in Liverpool and when we arrived the staff were absolutely superb. Everyone was slapping me on the back and saying "all the best". I went to bed feeling nervous, but in a good frame of mind. However I knew that it would all be for nothing if the judge and jury didn't believe my story.

THE NEXT MORNING, I rose early, got showered and dressed and went downstairs without having anything for breakfast. I just couldn't eat. Originally, the plan was to go to court by car, but we decided we'd walk since it was only a mile away and it would allow us to clear our heads. Little did we anticipate the media scrum that awaited us: there were cameramen on every street corner, but it soon became clear that they'd all assumed we would be driving. The very first photographer we went past didn't even recognise me. And so it went on. On every street corner there were photographers, but they never cottoned on. We couldn't help but raise a smile.

It was very different when we arrived at the courtroom, I've never seen so many cameras flashing. Ann had to leave me at that point: she wasn't allowed into court because she was a witness. As we parted she struggled to hold back her emotions. We kissed goodbye privately – the last thing we wanted were pictures of us together plastered all over the next day's papers. It was pretty emotional. Then I was alone.

Ann:
Saying goodbye just round the corner from the court was the single most draining experience of my life. It felt as if everything we'd been through came to bear on that one moment. I could not contain myself and cried my eyes out. I didn't want to let Dave go – in case I never got him back again.

Dave:
As I got to the court, a policeman told me he could get me in the back door to avoid the media hordes. I remember answering him, "No, I'm going to walk in the front – and I'm going to walk back out the front when it's over." He smiled at me, I think acknowledging my chutzpah.

Naturally I was extremely nervous, but not nearly as fraught as Ann who walked round the city centre – just as she had done all those months ago when I was first arrested. They do say the calmest place to be in a storm is the eye.

Ann:

It was pouring down with rain as I wandered around Liverpool, but as it was just coming up to Christmas everyone was doing their shopping. There was lots of laughter all around me, but I was wrapped up in my own little world. Tears flooded my eyes constantly. Every time I wiped them away more appeared. I couldn't control myself.

I remember Dave's mum ringing me and asking me how things were going. I couldn't tell her anything even though she was in a terrible state. There I was trying to calm her down even though I was equally tearful.

The court broke for lunch at noon so I returned and stood among all the reporters with an umbrella. No-one knew who I was – just someone waiting for word from the big case of the day. As Dave came through the rotating doors, the photographers flashed their cameras, but I quickly put the umbrella in front of one of them so he couldn't get his pictures.

In a way it was good I wasn't able to be in court – I'd have struggled to keep my cool and would surely have been tempted to shout out at the wrong time. But I was fascinated by every detail of what it was like and what was going on. I remember asking my sister, who was in there for every minute of the trial, what the jurors looked like. I think I thought they had to look normal to meet my approval. Strange things go through your head at times like that.

The sense of isolation was unbearable as I remained on the outside throughout everything Dave was going through: every time he went back into court in the coming days I was left on my own again.

Dave:

The thing I wasn't sure about when I got into the courtroom was where to sit. Something in my head said I'd be with my solicitor, like you see in the movies. I never realised I would be right at the very back, away from everybody. Stephen Pollard's number two Linzi McDonald was maybe four or five rows in front with nobody in between us. I was sitting on a bench by myself which, I soon found out, led directly down to the cells. That discovery sent a chill down my spine.

I knew what would be going through Ann's head, but for me it was a case of stiff upper lip and outward confidence. I was ready to do battle. The jury was asked whether they had any ties with me. It was just a formality, of course, but I swear many of them smiled at me as they took their seats, which was strangely unnerving. Then came the moment when I was asked to give my name and plea.

"David Jones, not guilty." I stated. They were the only words I was to utter throughout the whole process.

Right from the start I had prepared myself for the prosecution lawyer to have a real go at me, but when he began I felt almost as if he was on my side. It was as if he was working for me, not the CPS – a really odd sensation. He called me upstanding, said I'd never been involved with the police. In fact it seemed that everything he said about me was nice. His punchline was, "We have to prove that the defendant has a dark secret." That was the worst thing he said about me. I got the impression he did not believe I had done anything wrong, that he was simply going through the motions because he'd been employed to do a job. I speculated in my mind that he had been forced to continue on with a case that he knew he had no chance of winning because of the maniacal desire of the police to see me go down.

It was all so surreal.

Thoughts crossed my mind. What am I doing here? Why are all these people here? What's going to happen? When I came out for that first-day lunch break, it was so good to see Ann. We were all taken to Starbucks and I have to say it was like a party atmosphere. Jeff and Ian, the guys I had been to Portugal with and who had been inside the courtroom, kept insisting the prosecution didn't have a dog's chance. It really lightened the mood.

The prosecution barrister's opening address took most of the afternoon, although one thing that sticks in my mind was hearing that my accusers were in the cells below. I remember anticipating finally laying eyes on the people who had created my living hell by perpetrating a tissue of lies. As it happened I would not see them yet.

That first day seemed to fly by and that evening, in an effort to avoid watching ourselves on TV – I appeared to be the lead story on most of the early evening news programmes and popping up once or twice an hour on *Sky News* – Jeff suggested we go out to eat at a restaurant in Liverpool. We badly needed some food since we had hardly eaten the whole day.

Leaving the hotel coincided with another downpour, so we were hurrying along the street under umbrellas, heads down, when I heard Jeff say, under his breath, "Oh, f***."

I looked up and saw a man and woman walking towards us. I recognised the woman immediately. It was the Crown Prosecution Service officer who was dealing with the case against me. I had felt all along that she had been the driving force behind the incessant pursuit of me despite the total lack of corroborated evidence from credible witnesses. For me she stood for all that was wrong with the case which was being presented to the court about me. I had told Ann all about this woman over the months, but Ann had no idea what she looked like. I knew that Ann was still on an emotional knife edge and could overreact if I told her who it was walking towards us. I looked across at Ann and saw that she too had heard Jeff's comment. She looked up and then looked at me as if to say 'what?' She'd twigged there was something going on, but thankfully she didn't realise what until the woman and her companion had walked past, flashing a quick glance in my direction and saying "Good evening".

It was that look which clicked with Ann. She put two and two together right away, but thankfully she was too stunned to do anything about it. She turned to Jeff and asked, "Is that her?"

"Yes, that's her," he confirmed.

Ann turned round in a flash, hell-bent on letting this woman have a piece of her mind. We had to physically restrain her from doing so, but I could sympathise with her motives. Only a few hours earlier, as the clock ticked towards the appointed start time for the trial, this CPS officer had sat opposite me in court with a big smirk on her face. At one point she actually nodded at me as if to say hello with a broad, knowing grin which smugly said 'I've got you'.

That encounter put me off any thought of food and it took a long time to calm Ann down. Not much had happened that first day, but without question the tension was mounting.

NO SMOKE, NO FIRE

I HAD BEEN informed from the outset that the case could last over two weeks, so I was prepared for the long haul. But ultimately the trial collapsed in under four days. We had a whole list of people lined up as defence witnesses, but none of them were needed as one by one my accusers melted away. Before the jury was even sworn in seven charges were dropped as one of my four alleged 'victims' pulled out from giving evidence against me, while a second failed to show up. This man, who was arguably their key witness and who I shall call Donald as I am not allowed to name him for legal reasons, was an ex-convict. The judge gave the prosecution time to persuade him to attend, but by the third day it became apparent that Donald had got cold feet. It seemed that he was not prepared to go through with the lies on oath in case it earned him more time inside.

The transsexual arsonist did take the stand to give evidence against me. This was my first chance to see the whites of the eyes of one of these people who had made up such disgusting lies about me. This was a person who was serving a prison sentence and who, we had discovered, had undergone a psychiatric report six months earlier in which he mentioned everyone who had supposedly abused him at Clarence

House. There was no mention of me in it. This was, we had also found, the same person who had written a letter to a social worker asking to be moved back to Clarence House since that was where he had the happiest months of his time in care and in it he mentioned how much he liked the staff. Only when this person saw my picture in the paper did things miraculously appear to come flooding back.

Just seeing the way this creature operated in court made my stomach churn and I found myself loathing him with a vengeance. At one point in his evidence he told the court he was three-quarters of the way to becoming a full woman. When I heard that, fuelled by the stress I was under and the hatred I felt towards this person who was purveying lies about me in court, under my breath I said to myself, "Yeah, and I'll finish the job for you." The guard who had brought him up from the cells was standing next to me, heard what I said and I had to bite my lip when he whispered to me, "And I'll help you."

The final witness, the boy who Dina had shown such kindness to that Christmas and who I shall call Mickey, was serving a long jail sentence for armed robbery. He also had the gall to appear in the witness box. I listened incredulously, anger boiling inside me, as he told the court of some disgusting things he alleged I had done to him at Clarence House. The detail he gave was stomach-churning. I won't go into it, but it sickened me to think that anyone could be capable of such horrendous acts, let alone make these lies up to falsely accuse me.

The comforting factor was that we knew this person's evidence was fatally flawed from the start. We could show that I was in fact on holiday at the time he claimed I had committed these vile acts. Not only that, but he had claimed in his statement to the police that he had never returned to Clarence House after the alleged abuse he suffered at my hands. In fact, we had learned from records that he had gone back to Clarence House directly after the date in question, and willingly. When these facts were put to him and he was pressed about the accuracy of his evidence, my accuser began to falter.

My barrister, Henry Globe (who went on to become the Recorder of Liverpool), tore his story to pieces. Mickey was something of a cocksure guy and that would prove to be his and the case's downfall. As Henry built up to asking him about this issue of returning to the Home, Mickey made a glib comment about how he knew what he was going to be asked next. The wily Henry asked him how he knew and Mickey responded that police officers had visited him to warn him that my team had uncovered this hole in his story. At that point, Mickey, hoisted by his own petard, admitted to having concocted his evidence and named the police officers who visited him in prison and told him what to expect to be asked. Unfortunately legal requirements prevent me from doing so here, although I feel extremely aggrieved that I am not allowed to identify those who I believe were pushing the boundaries of the law in order to see me convicted. However I wil not lower myself to their level by transgressing those boundaries myself.

As it happened this revelation coincided with the end of the morning session. Henry Globe requested statements from the officers who had been named by Mickey. They arrived, denying any such meeting had ever taken place. Before the afternoon session got underway the prosecution indicated they wanted to suspend Mickey's evidence. The judge, David Clarke, wasn't at all pleased, cleared the jury and gallery, and told the prosecution in no uncertain terms to go away and consider if they wished to continue. After all, if the jury believed the evidence this witness was giving, then someone was at fault for putting words into his mouth. If, on the other hand, no-one had said anything to him, then the man was lying and in contempt of court.

The next incredible event to reveal itself emerged almost immediately. Another barrister unconnected with our case witnessed one of the senior CPS lawyers involved in my case hugging a witness in the cells below the courtroom, and did his professional duty and informed the judge. It is, after all, wholly inappropriate and unprofessional to do that sort of thing. I never met the barrister in question, but I wish to place my thanks to him on record. When pressed in court about this, the CPS lawyer claimed they had been hugging the witness to 'comfort' him, but it didn't wash. The case against me had been totally discredited.

Many months later I publicly stated that those who made the accusations against me should crawl back into their prison cells and make sure they never walk in front of my car headlights on a dark night. I regret saying that. It was a statement borne out of fury and resent-ment. I hope, though, it is understandable why in an unguarded moment I might say such a thing, and that I can be excused that one public indiscretion after months of private hell. It did, however, lower me to the level of those who accused me. Thankfully it was only words. I could never actually begin to contemplate doing such a thing.

The case against me was clearly crumbling and I grew more and more heartened by the minute. During one break we had bumped into some of the police and their legal team in the lift and Jeff kept telling me loudly how well the case was going from my point of view right in front of them all. He lapped up every second of that ride and they all looked totally embarrassed. And rightly so, for what subsequently happened showed their case up for what it was: a complete farce.

On the morning of day four, with no sign of Donald, with the other witnesses discredited and with the revelations about witness-coaching leaving their case in tatters, the prosecution approached the bench and submitted that no further evidence was to be offered. The judge retired to make a decision. I was taken into a back room to sit and wait for the outcome. I was told it would go one of two ways. Either it would be thrown out entirely, or there would be a retrial. Suddenly I could sense the end of my ordeal approaching rapidly. It felt like light was shining into my world at last.

"No retrial," I said. "It gets done today, it gets finished today." I could hardly bear the tension which was gripping me. I could smell, taste, feel freedom. I wanted it so badly. Henry Globe and Stephen Pollard were pleading my case with the Judge and I had every faith in them. I sat for what seemed like an eternity. Waiting. Hoping.

THE DOOR OPENED, banging against the wall, jolting me from my daydream – the most pleasant I'd had in 18 months since this whole nightmare had begun. Henry walked over to me, leant across the table that I was sitting behind and informed me with a smile on his face that the judge had made his decision.

"The case has been dismissed," he said. "All charges."

I collapsed forwards and felt the elation rush over me.

"Yeeesss!"

Henry told me that in throwing the case out Judge David Clarke was apparently absolutely disgusted with how the police and CPS had behaved – so much so that he wanted to know what I would like him to say in my defence in his summing up. "In all my years as barrister, I have never heard this before," said Henry, flabbergasted. "Judges just don't do that sort of thing. It's unprecedented, Dave."

I didn't know how to respond, my emotions were in turmoil and I knew I might not be able to contain my disgust for what had happened to me, so suggested the Judge simply say whatever words he thought fit.

Ann:

When Stephen called to tell me to come to the courtroom immediately, I couldn't bear to ask whether it was bad news. Throughout the hearing, part of me had been terrified Dave might be convicted. It had been my big fear all along. After all, there are numerous precedents of miscarriages of justice, people convicted and then acquitted years later. Even now I find it too painful to discuss how I would have coped with the rest of my life if things had gone against us. I entered the courtroom in trepidation, hoping beyond hope that things would go our way.

Dave:

The jury were directed by the Judge to find me not guilty on four of the fourteen charges and then he told them they could not return verdicts on the remainder of the charges due to the prosecution failing to provide evidence. I was genuinely touched when, in his closing speech, he cong-ratulated me on the "restraint and dignity" with which I had faced the charges. The whole gallery spontaneously erupted with approval and joy.

Then came the words that will live with me for ever: "No doubt there will be people who are going to think there is no smoke without fire," His Honour Judge David Clarke QC said. "I can do nothing about that except to say such an attitude would be wrong. No wrong-doing whatsoever on your part has been established." In other words, there *was* no smoke and there *was* no fire.

Ann:
I felt a flood of sheer elation when the Judge dismissed the case and said such noble things about Dave. All I wanted was to give Dave a hug and for us to go back to our lives and forget all of this nightmare.

Dave:
"It's all over," I said. "It's finished." We embraced and Ann burst into tears.

And she wasn't the only one. Everyone was screaming and shouting, it was total mayhem. When we eventually emerged from the courtroom after a good time congratulating each other, the news had already hit the press. I was even being slapped on the back by some of the ushers and people involved in totally unconnected cases. All our friends and family then went back to the hotel to start the party, except for me and Ann who went to Henry Globe's chambers for some celebratory champagne with Stephen and Linzi. We then walked back to the Crowne Plaza, and as we did so we walked past the Starbucks coffee shop that had served as our meeting point during the case. Everyone spontaneously piled out to greet us, then a bus stopped and everyone who got off came and shook my hand – even the driver. Cars were beeping and a walk that should have taken 15 minutes took nearly an hour. It was a bit like one of those tickertape home-coming parades. I felt on top of the world and as we walked into the hotel, there was a massive cheer.

As the celebrations got into full swing, my phone started ringing with people wanting to offer congratulations. The first person who called was my former Everton playing colleague Bryan Hamilton. It was a terrific gesture since he himself had only just been sacked as manager of Norwich City. It really says something about Bryan's character that he bothered to get in touch given all that was going on in his life.

As far as I can remember, the next person who phoned was Bill Kenwright, the theatrical entrepreneur and Everton chairman. I've known Bill since I was 15 and he was absolutely delighted with the outcome. From then on my phone never stopped ringing.

It wasn't just my friends and colleagues who were pleased I had been acquitted of all charges. During the trial I had been urged by Stephen Pollard to concentrate on what was being said and not to look at the jury. I found that difficult sometimes, especially as I wanted to see what their reaction was. I don't know why, but I had a warm feeling towards them from day one. Maybe I was wrong, but as the 12 jury members were dismissed, I swear one of them, as he was walking past me, gave me the thumbs up as if to say justice had been done.

But it might not have been. History is full of innocent men and women who have been sent to jail for crimes they did not commit. I am not too naïve to realise that it could easily have happened to me. Before my trial began, relatively few people understood how a former care worker could possibly be facing more than 20 counts of physical and sexual abuse from four separate accusers, and claim he was innocent and that all of the allegations were totally false. But by the time the trial collapsed, practically everyone knew the explanation.

Which only adds to the chilling nature of the whole episode – having gone through what I have, in my opinion it is wholly wrong that convicted criminals can be allowed to swear solemn oaths on the Bible and give testimonies in open court which could send decent men to prison. All the more so, in my opinion at least, that they are encouraged to do so by a police operation more interested in hitting targets, or needing a high profile result, than in the truth. Those officers who so doggedly pursued me still feature in my thoughts on a regular basis. They *must* have reached a point when they knew that they had a flimsy case at best . . . and yet they continued to hound me. In my opinion, the case should never have been brought to trial. That, clearly, was also the Judge's opinion and in his closing speech he had addressed the very thing I had been worried about – that mud would stick no matter what.

Stephen Pollard told me something that I have never forgotten and never will: that in his 25 years in the job he had never been so convinced of anyone's innocence. More witnesses than you can imagine had volunteered to give evidence on my behalf. Thankfully they were never needed. But to me they were all heroes.

What still rankles with me today is that under the Sexual Offences (Amendment) Act 1992 I am not allowed to name the four people who gave false statements to the police accusing me of these hideous crimes. I find it astonishing and absolutely disgraceful that, incredibly, the legislation affords total anonymity to anyone against whom it is alleged that sexual abuse has taken place – even if they have made up that allegation themselves. I can, of course, understand the need for genuine sufferers of abuse to remain unidentified, especially if they are still children, but that was just not the case here. Why is there no provision for those who concocted these horrendous false allegations about me to be named and shamed? Why was I not afforded that same anonymity? Why do I have to live with the after-effects of the trial still, a decade on, when my name was totally cleared, while my accusers can never suffer for their crimes? Why does this crass law continue to protect those who have lied in other similar cases? This seems to me a scandalous anomaly, a loophole, which needs to be closed, and soon.

Equally, not being able to name the people who I feel hounded me long after they must have known that the allegations were utter rubbish, angers me greatly. They sought to destory my life and yet have faced few, if any, repercussions themselves. Incredibly, the person who admitted 'hugging' the witness, after initially being suspended from duty, was cleared of any wrong doing by an internal investigation. I find that amazing, but not as astounding as the fact that one of those people now holds a very senior position in the Crown Prosecution Service. How on earth can that have happened? Is that how we reward incompetence and such lack of judgement in this country? It's a disgrace.

In writing this book I have revisited the feelings and emotions of that 18-month period which climaxed in that wonderful day when the charges against me were dismissed. Over that time I developed an intense hatred of the scumbags who had perpetrated the horrific lies. And yet I ended up blaming the police far more than my accusers. Why? Because they allowed themselves to be blinkered by their pursuit of me.

Did I believe in the judicial system beforehand? Absolutely. Do I now? Absolutely not. I have to say that I would never tar all police officers with the same brush. Far from it. Indeed I have relatives and friends in the service. But in my opinion the relevant department of Merseyside Police didn't do their job properly. Their incompetence, and blindness to the blatantly obvious, beggared belief. There was even one moment during the trial when one of the CPS legal team demanded that Ann, my wife, be removed from the gallery because, as one of my witnesses, she wasn't allowed to see any of the proceedings. That would have been quite correct if Ann had indeed been sitting in on another part of the trial – but Ann wasn't there. It was her sister that the not-so-eagle-eyed CPS representative had spotted. They just hadn't a clue.

In a way I'm now glad the case went to court to prove what a total farce the whole thing was. It took away any doubt in anyone's mind.

Ann:
I called Dot to let her know the news and the first thing she did was to go round to the girls' schools and ask the teachers to let them out for the day. We had decided to drive straight home from Liverpool so we could see the kids. Initially, though, the schools got the wrong end of the stick and thought Dave had been found guilty. Chloe actually told us that her heart sank when her teacher told her to go and see the headmaster. She almost passed out and it wasn't until she saw Dot outside that she learned what had happened. She burst into tears, as Danielle did when she found out.

Dave:
When we arrived home the next day, the kids came rushing down the drive to greet us. They had been waiting by the windows and couldn't wait to see us. We all embraced in a massive group hug. It was, as you can imagine, the best hug I've ever had.

Ann and I decided that the following night we'd have a big party. We wanted to thank everyone who had supported us, so about 40 of us went to Regina's restaurant in Botley. Stuart and Kath Gray were there, so was John Sainty and his wife Christine and Dennis Rofe, anyone who had done anything to help us. Stuart in fact made a speech, as did I. There were once again tears in my eyes when I thanked everyone for believing in us. It really had been the one thing that kept us going. John Sainty's daughter Jo, a professional singer, entertained us for most of a fabulous evening. It was undoubtedly one of the best nights of my life.

AFTERMATH

I CAN'T STRESS enough how thankful I am to the friends who stood by me during the toughest time of my life. There are too many to mention all of them, but they know who they are and how much I appreciate them.

Top of the list has to be my business partner Phil Jones. We became friends with Phil and his wife Jenny when Lea played football as a junior. Phil is a mad Evertonian, in fact his car registration is EFC. He still lives up in Formby and we get together as often as we can. By pure coincidence, Phil lived next door to the Chief of Merseyside police at the time of my case and tried constantly to persuade him to drop it. When that didn't happen, he got increasingly angry. He just couldn't comprehend it. One of the more amusing anecdotes that I recall involving Phil took place at the Magistrates' Court that sent me for trial. Phil and one of his friends, Tommy, decided they were not going to have me sitting on my own, so came downstairs from the gallery and plonked themselves next to me. You should have seen the look of amazement on the faces on the prosecution. Just as they were about to say 'You can't sit there', the Magistrates entered, everyone rose and that was the end of it. They didn't even notice the pair of them sitting there.

Phil and Jenny became my biggest allies – and to be fair to many others I had a lot of fantastic support. I would have trusted Phil with my life. He would not hear a bad word against me. He lost friends, or people he thought were friends, in going overboard supporting me. When people would come out with the old no smoke without fire line, Phil would shoot them down in flames.

Jeff Mahe, the policeman who I have referred to many times already, was another trusted ally. He helped me understand the legal procedure both at the Magistrates' Court, and then Crown Court. He was also the man who introduced me to Ray Wyre. But what I am even more grateful for is how he handled my actual court appearances, getting me in and out of the building in ways that meant I wouldn't have to face the cameras.

As well as all my friends, the walls of our house had been festooned with hundreds of letters of support received before the case. Now even more cards congratulating me came flooding in, virtually covering the whole place. It was wonderful to know I had such good will from so many people who I had never met. It felt like there were also just as many people who offered support from families of those who were in the same predicament as me, all totally innocent. That was when I first realised I was becoming many people's shining light, not something I was entirely comfortable with it has to be said. I was primarily interested in my own case and my family. It was enough to cope with.

However, I do realise just what my predicament meant to other families in the same boat. Ann loves to recall the story of the little boy who came up to her at the Magistrates' Court before my case went to trial and asked whether she was Dave Jones' wife. He couldn't have been more than six or seven. When she said "yes", he told her his daddy had already gone to prison and he was there with his mum and others to support me and protest about Operation Care. Ann just wanted to scoop the little boy up and cuddle him.

Another story, again from my appearance at the Magistrates' Court, was equally memorable. As we were approaching the court in separate cars – me with Jeff in one and Ann behind with the family – it was clear that hundreds of cameramen and media were waiting for us. Jeff had a way of dealing with this. We were still 300 yards away when he called one of his friends in the courtroom and asked whether he could usher me into a side entrance to avoid the hordes. It was a hugely courageous thing to do. Jeff was wearing a bright florescent yellow bomber jacket, which stood out like a sore thumb. Being a policeman, he was obviously putting his own situation in jeopardy by helping me without any of his superiors knowing.

As we got out of the cars, one of the snappers shouted "Here he is". Like bees to a honey pot they swarmed up the street towards us. I think Jeff's jacket may have been what attracted them because later on he was on virtually every television news programme, in fact taking up even more screen time than me.

As I squeezed into the back entrance, Ann had a somewhat colourful confrontation with one of the snappers. As the photographer charged to try and get pictures of me, he aggressively shoved everyone out of the way. But not Ann. As he tried to get past her, she sidestepped and stood in his way. He tripped and fell to floor in a crumpled heap, throwing every possible expletive in Ann's direction. She just smiled at him as if to say, "That's for being so rude."

As for Jeff, the next day when he went into work all his mates had seen his picture in the papers and his face on TV. His boss took a somewhat tongue-in-cheek view. "If you are going to sneak someone in the back entrance to a courtroom, don't bloody wear a fluorescent yellow bomber jacket!" was what he told Jeff. Or words to that effect.

GETTING BACK TO the aftermath of my trial, I held the customary press conference, but then decided to do just one separate television appearance, one radio show and give one newspaper interview. There were so many things I wanted to say, but I knew we'd be inundated with everyone wanting a piece of me and I just wanted to get on with my life.

After all enough tragedy and injustice had visited my family – my court case, that fairground accident Chloe suffered, not to mention Georgia being struck down with osteomyelitis, Lea breaking a bone in his back and being forced to give up football and, worst of all, that terrible railway accident that killed my brother-in-law Peter and the lethal brain tumour that killed Ann's nephew. As I have said earlier in the book, I'm certain my father's illness was also brought on a by a broken heart. It turned me inside out at his funeral knowing he would almost certainly still be alive without the allegations.

Could one family suffer much more pain? I wouldn't wish what happened to me even on my worst enemy. Adjusting to life in a Merseyside care home with little relevant experience after having my career cut short by injury had been hard enough for a man used to performing in front of packed terraces, but being accused over a decade later of doing unspeakable things while I was there, then seeing it spiral out of control, was the ultimate sickening nightmare. Wrong place, wrong time. Now I was determined to make up for lost time.

Ann:

I never ever doubted Dave's innocence throughout our 18-month ordeal. If anything our relationship grew stronger. We have our arguments like most couples, but we have a marriage built on trust. I have known Dave for more than 40 years. He says I know him better than he does himself.

Perhaps the saddest thing about the whole process is that Dave and I have always loved children. Our houses have always been full of kids. At every opportunity he would always be with his own c6ildren. He was there at all their births and I was a registered child minder for the best part of ten years

I always thought that the police were trying to drive a wedge between us as they pursued Dave, but in fact they could never have done so. They never twigged the fact that I had been working at Clarence House during the period that Dave was supposed to be abusing kids so not only did I have the knowledge of what my husband was really like, but I had actually been working in the same place and had never come across any hint of there being a problem. I knew he could not have done any of the things of which he was accused and so was always totally behind his fight to clear his name. It did not stop me, however, from having extremely black moments when I worried about what might happen, about how both Dave and I would cope if things went wrong and about how Dave could become the real victim in all of this.

Dave:

When we originally decided the time was right to write this book and explain to everyone what we had been through, Ann wanted to talk about those grim inner fears she had and explain to people just how daunting that empty void is when you contemplate life on your own, in shame, feeling dirty. But when it came to it she couldn't bring herself to lay all those raw emotions on the table. Even ten years on it's too painful, too close to the bone.

What pleases me now, looking back, is that because I have managed to come through the storm I can help others. I can bring my experience to bear and assist them. Not so long ago, I went to do a talk at Derby County FC and was asked the question by a worried youth team coach, what should we do if we are falsely accused? Find the best lawyer was my answer. For I have learned from bitter experience that for this type of accusation in this country you are guilty until proved innocent, even though it is supposed to be the other way round. Once you are tarred with that brush, it sticks.

We didn't know it at the time, but my case sparked a series of retrials of innocent care workers wrongly convicted on the basis of questionable evidence because of the disgraceful policy of trawling. How interesting that after my acquittal, two men, Basil Williams Rigby (the father of that little boy who had spoken to Ann) and Michael Lawson, who had both been given long prison terms, were freed by the court of appeal after witnesses in my case had their evidence, which had also put those two gentlemen inside, discredited. How interesting, too, that their lawyers claimed at the first trials they had been originally convicted on uncorroborated evidence of complainants who may have been motivated by the possibility of compensation.

How interesting, too, that Merseyside Police closed Operation Care.

It's a sobering thought that without my own acquittal, these and other innocent men may never have been freed.

STARTING OVER

AT LAST WE were no longer living on egg shells. The nightmare was over and we began to feel as if we could move on with the rest of our lives. It was Christmas time, although it felt as if we'd done all our celebrating already, so we just had a quiet family party, taking advantage of being unusually free over the normally frantic festive period for football people. Since the case had been dismissed and the celebrations had died down people had been telling me to take a break, but they were missing the point. I'd already had one. I was chomping at the bit.

I still had no job, of course, although to be fair to Rupert Lowe it has to be said he did have the good grace to write to me after the trial was over and say how pleased he was about the outcome. So the first thing I wanted to do professionally was get back into football management, though I had no idea at what level I would be able to achieve this given all that had gone on and my enforced year or so out of the game. Quite frankly I was prepared to start at the bottom. It didn't really bother me given what I'd been through. I'd proved myself before and would do so again.

We had spent around £400,000 clearing my name which meant I was now around £1.4m out of pocket since the allegations had hit me. That is an awful lot of money even for a Premier League manager back in 2000 – a financial hit. But even before the court case, a few clubs had been sounding me out. From two weeks before the trial to two weeks after about a dozen or so clubs had contacted me. One chairman even rang me up two days after the case and apologised for taking so long to get in touch! I wasn't prepared for the amount of interest shown in me, though Ann was convinced that after what I had endured for the previous 18 months running a football team would be a doddle.

Within three to four weeks of being acquitted I was offered three jobs, all within an hour of being interviewed, at Championship clubs. What particularly pleased me was that none of the chairmen involved so much as once mentioned the court case. I was suddenly in big demand.

Premier League Derby had already approached me via Jim Smith. They were looking for a replacement for the Bald Eagle who was planning to step down at the end of the season. The problem was I couldn't wait that long. I wanted in now, and with the Christmas and New Year period traditionally being a time when boards of underperforming clubs sack managers and look for saviours, I hoped I could find a club. Anyway, I needed to find a job quickly for simple financial reasons.

The first Championship club, who wanted me to start there and then, were Barnsley and I agreed to meet the chairman John Dennis at a motorway junction from where he would escort me to his house just before Christmas. Unfortunately that morning there was a huge accident on the M1 and I was no less than three and a half hours late for the appointment. I kept in contact with John by phone and, bless him, he waited for me the whole time without so much as a single question. He wanted me that badly – even before we had met. When we eventually got to his house, John sold me a fantastic pitch. He had a contract already laid out for me on the kitchen table under the assumption, I guess, that I would simply sign it. He then – wait for it – locked the door behind me and told me I wasn't leaving until I put pen to paper. Obviously it was half in jest – John was a really lovely man.

But I knew that I had other fish to fry. I had already got word from my agent that Norwich were interested in me and had arranged to go and see them too. I told John I couldn't take the gamble of jumping in straight away and needed the opportunity to meet with Norwich. He replied that I wasn't going anywhere. I pretty much had to fight my way out of the house. That's Yorkshire hospitality for you!

What I hadn't told John, although I'm not sure why, was that Wolves wanted to see me too. Jez Moxey, the chief executive at Molineux, gave me an address in London at which to meet him and another of the directors. As I walked towards the address I'd been given, who should come walking the other way but Dave 'Harry' Bassett, the man who had just been sacked by Barnsley! Harry, being Harry, didn't tell me where he'd been, but it was pretty obvious he'd been to see Moxey. I told him, by contrast, where I was off to. What did I have to lose? It wasn't as if I was the only one being interviewed, others were bound to have been called as well. Harry could easily have pointed me in the right direction but he didn't. Instead he just wished me all the best and carried on walking.

I soon realised that Harry knew exactly what he was doing as he'd obviously been through the same level of farce as I was about to experience. When I got to where I'd been sent, I knocked at the door and a flustered woman appeared as if to say 'Not again!' They'd only sent me to the wrong address. They were actually next door. Not a very good start.

Anyway I ended up being interviewed for a couple of hours and for some reason I didn't think it went that well. I can't explain why. They went on about the youth policy and asked if I knew all the players at the club. I phoned Ann and said I really wasn't sure how I'd done. I didn't know Jez at the time and told her that I thought he was a bit cold towards me.

Next I was off to Norwich. I was determined not to sell myself short in making my decision as to which job to take and to make sure I was taking the right step. For some reason Delia Smith wanted Ann to come with me, which I thought was a bit odd, but that's apparently the way Delia does things, she likes to meet the wives and hold the interview at her house. Norwich is obviously quite a way from Southampton, about a four-hour journey, but we didn't bother to eat much on the way as we presumed – who wouldn't? – that we'd be well fed when we got there; plus the meeting was set for lunchtime. When we arrived, all the Norwich board were sitting in Delia's lounge. It was pretty informal. In the end they didn't ask Ann much except for how she'd feel about going all the way from Southampton to Norwich. I recall she replied something along the lines of Norwich being a doddle compared with Hong Kong where I had played after leaving Coventry. They all roared with laughter.

The interview went really well. I have to say they were fantastic people. Delia said they'd have a board meeting, come to a decision and let me know within a couple of days.

As we came out of the house a raging snowstorm had just started. We began the long drive home. It was pelting down, with terrible visibility, and we were starving, absolutely ravenous. We'd been at Delia Smith's house about three hours and hadn't eaten the cordon bleu lunch we'd anticipated. All we'd had was a mince pie – it was just before Christmas after all – and a cup of tea! In hindsight it's our own fault. We should have said something. I'm sure Delia would have rustled up something fabulous for us.

As we drove through the blizzard, Barnsley Chairman John Dennis called. His first words, in his thick Yorkshire accent, were: "It's a bloody long way to get to Norwich son, isn't it?" It was clear he was not prepared to take no for an answer, but I had kind of made up my mind that I would go to Norwich. I can tell you now, and I've never said this before publicly, that if Delia had offered me the job there and then while I was still at her house, I'd have taken it – and I'd have kept my word. There would have been no Wolves.

But as it happened Norwich hesitated too long. In the space of the next few minutes the destination of my next managerial job was all but settled. We were driving across East Anglia still looking for something to eat, when I received two more phone calls in quick succession that were to shape the rest of my career. First on the line was Jez Moxey asking me how I thought my interview with him went. I was honest with him, but surprised and delighted to learn that the feeling apparently wasn't mutual. He said he thought it went really well. They wanted to see me again, this time with owner Sir Jack Hayward. I couldn't believe it and was in a state of shock. Wolves are a massive club, and I imagined going there with the history and the fan base. Now I had more than an inkling I was first choice. After all you don't meet someone like Sir Jack if you are not high on the list.

No sooner had I put the phone down to Jez than Delia called, offering me the Norwich job. She didn't know it, but she had missed the boat by a split second. I told her I couldn't make a decision because I had someone else to see. She tried to persuade me there and then, saying they originally weren't going to make a decision for a couple of days but had been so impressed with me that they had decided I was the man for the job as soon as I had walked out the door. If she had called me before rather than after Jez, I'd have become the manager of the Canaries instead of the Wolves. That's what football is like. You simply never know what's in store.

I'd travelled up to Barnsley a few days earlier with no job. Now, in the space of 20 minutes, I had three — alright two-and-a-half — jobs. Even with the snow piling down we roared home. Before we arrived, John Dennis called me again. This time, I told him about my prospective meeting with Sir Jack at Wolves. Forthright as ever, John's exact words were, "Why do you want to work for that old fart?!" He and Sir Jack are actually good mates, but his next comment was deadly serious: "Name your price." I couldn't. It wasn't just about the money. It was about what was best for me and the temptation of Wolves was too good to turn down.

RUNNING WITH WOLVES

WOLVERHAMPTON WANDERERS ARE a massive club. The potential at Molineux is frightening. The club had been in the doldrums for years, even falling as low as the Fourth Division in the mid-1980s and had been stuck in the second tier of English football for over a decade. Five managers had come and gone in that time, failing to lead Wolves back into the promised land of the Premier League. I knew I could do it. I knew this was the right challenge for me. They were close to the bottom of the Championship at the time, just a point above the relegation zone, but they had good players, so the first job would be to restore confidence and get them up the table.

I met Sir Jack Hayward in London in a massive boardroom at a hotel. It was like a ballroom with a table in the middle. Sir Jack asked me about my life and football. He never even mentioned the case. I was actually perfectly happy to talk about it, but didn't need to. Jez had told me before I even went into the room that the job was mine, which obviously relaxed me. I accepted it there and then and then phoned up the other two clubs to give them the news.

It was New Year's Eve and I didn't tell Ann I had got the job until I got home. I just walked into the house with a big beaming smile on my face. It was wonderful to be able to do that after all that we had been through.

We normally have a party at our house on New Year's Eve, but this year we hadn't planned anything because of my interviews. My mum was staying with us and so was Ann's sister Dot. To celebrate, Ann looked through the Yellow Pages for restaurants, but, phoning round, could not find a table at such late notice. She came across one that had availability and was asked how many the table was for. I quickly phoned round my former Southampton coaching staff with whom we were still good friends to see who was free. Denis Rofe, Stuart Gray and John Sainty were not doing anything and we booked this table for 16 of us for around 9 o'clock. It was already 7.45pm, so I rushed around getting ready, phoning friends and family to tell them about my new job as I did so. It made us late.

Just before 9pm, while I was still getting changed, I received a phone call from Denis Rofe: "Dave I'm outside the restaurant but it's all closed up," he said. "I'm banging on the door and no-one is answering."

Some frantic phoning and googling told us that the restaurant outside which Denis and his wife Sue were standing had practically, but not quite, the same name as the one Ann had booked. The restaurant Ann had told everyone to go to wasn't the one she had booked.

Worse was to follow. When Denis found it, the right restaurant was in the docks and hardly the kind of place you wanted to spend New Year's Eve. The real pits. In fact, an absolute dive. No wonder they could fit us in.

So Denis started combing Southampton High Street, heading into each and every restaurant asking if they could fit in a table for 16. The rest of us waited at home all dressed up with nowhere to go. Eventually Denis and Sue found this particular restaurant, which they'd been to quite often. Initially the owner gave the same negative response they'd received everywhere else – full to the hilt. But when Denis informed them that the table was for my impromptu party, the guy immediately said, "In that case . . . clear the tables."

It turned into an hysterical evening. We had the best New Year's Eve bash ever. The whole place was bouncing. Everyone in there knew who I was and were so happy for me. We all ended up dancing on the tables. It was an exhilarating and incredible night.

THE NEXT DAY, New Year's Day, however worse for wear I was, Wolves were playing at Burnley and I'd told Jez I'd go to the game just to watch. News of my appointment hadn't yet been made public and coaches John Ward and Terry Connor were looking after the side. Wolves won the game 1-0, but I didn't go into the dressing room afterwards to introduce myself because I felt it wasn't right to do so. John had set the team up so it was his day.

After the Wolves contingent had left Turf Moor, I thought I'd go and have a drink with Burnley manager Stan Ternent, who was a mate of mine. I walked across the pitch to the manager's office. As soon as I entered, Stan said to me, and these were his exact words, "You bastard, you've got the job. I know you have because I've never bleedin' beaten you!" And he hadn't. He'd never beaten me in head-to-head games. Burnley were flying at the time, but I was the curse of Stan again even though I was not officially the manager.

I was formally appointed and introduced as the new manager of Wolves on 3 January 2001. After all the press interviews I immediately got down to the serious business of deciding what I should do in terms of my staff at Wolves. I'm not the kind of manager who blindly takes staff with me from club to club. I tend to go and assess what's already there first. I felt the club needed a new chief scout, so I brought in a guy called George Foster who had a good reputation. Otherwise I kept the existing staff in place. As with all managerial changes, they had all been worried about their jobs and were relieved when I told them I didn't work that way. If they were good at what they did, there was job for them. I wouldn't be making any decisions until I knew what the chemistry was like between us.

My immediate thought on meeting the players was that Wolves simply had too many of them. They were coming out of your ears. I knew I'd have to trim.

My first game in charge was away at Nottingham Forest in the FA Cup, which we won the game 1-0 and Adam Proudlock scored.

The night before the game, I quickly realised what I let myself in for. The hotel we'd been booked into was the absolute pits, freezing cold with awful rooms and equally awful food. Not the kind of place a team with such an illustrious history should be spending the night before a game, let alone a cup tie against Midlands rivals. That was something that was going to have to change straight away.

When I got off the bus, the press were everywhere. After all it was my first game back. The reception I got from the Wolves fans at the game was amazing. The whole touchline was a mass of photographers. They must have been five deep. God only knows what my subs on the bench must have been thinking.

I adapted like a duck to water even though I was commuting from Southampton while we looked for somewhere to live. I stayed in a hotel during the week and returned home after the weekend game. We quickly started picking up points in the league and in fact got within a decent shout of the play-offs by the end of the campaign four months later. I told the staff there was a momentum going and we had a chance if we kept it going, but right at the crux of the season we went on a losing streak of three or four games and fell short. I couldn't quite fathom out what had happened, but I soon found out.

There's a lot that never comes out publicly when you're a football manager and this is one such story. Right at the end of the season I discovered that at Christmas (just before I was appointed and halfway through the season) a large number of the squad had booked a holiday together to Las Vegas – departing the day after the last scheduled league game. In other words, they had no intention of ever really trying to get to the play-offs, which would scupper their plans as they'd have to stick around for another two or three weeks.

One of the players, Paul Butler, who had joined on loan from Sunderland before I became manager, but who I then signed permanently, came to see me and told me about it. Buts was concerned about the situation and rightly so. These men were supposed to be professional footballers. I was absolutely livid.

It showed the kind of mentality the club had at the time and I made a decision there and then – call it harsh if you will – than none of the players who had booked that holiday would be at the club the following season.

None of them yet knew that I knew. As soon as that last game of the campaign against QPR was out of the way, I told them they would have to come back two days later for a close-season debriefing as we'd crumbled at the final hurdle and I wanted to make sure we started the new season on the front foot. At this point the players concerned had no option but to tell me what they were up to. I tore a strip off the miscreants in front of everyone and left them worrying for their futures. It was a major marker in the sand for me.

Yes, a lot of them were still under contract, but over the coming months I shifted them out one way or the other. There was no way they were ever going to play for me again. I was backed 100 per cent by Sir Jack and Jez, who were equally shocked when I told them about the situation. And when it came down to it many of the players weren't good enough anyway. They'd finished 12th in the table, just seven points above the relegation zone. I was not going to stand for that level of under-achievement in my first full season in charge.

And I was proved right. A lot of wheeling and dealing, including moving on all those who had crossed me and others who I felt just were not good enough, provided me with almost a new first team, including the key signings of Kenny Miller, Colin Cameron, Shaun Newton and Nathan Blake. The 2001/02 season was a far better campaign and saw us reach the brink of elation by finishing third, just three points off an automatic promotion place. We had a really strong team and should have gone up automatically. What we lacked was any knowledge of how to win those key, vital games at the business end of the season. Three times before Wolves had been in the play-offs and three times they had come up short. It was a mental problem.

After beating Gillingham 2-0 in early March we led the table, eight points ahead of second-placed Manchester City and a further two clear of West Bromwich Albion. There were only nine games to go and somehow we surrendered that lead to miss out on automatic promotion to, of all people, the Baggies from just down the road. West Brom had gone on an incredible late run to win eight of their last 10 games and nick second spot from us. We won just two of those last nine matches and so went into the play-offs as a team bang out of form.

With the words of Sir Jack still ringing in my ears – "Get me promotion son, and you'll never have to work for the rest of your life" – we faced Norwich in the semi-finals. The irony of the two clubs who had been fighting over my services just 17 months earlier facing each other in this duel to the death was not lost on me. Nigel Worthington had been handed the reins at Norwich and had done an outstanding job with them. We lost the first leg at Carrow Road 3-1, conceding a vital last minute goal by Malky Mackay. We huffed and puffed in the return game, but didn't score until the 77th minute and then couldn't get the second goal we needed. We won 1-0, but bowed out 3-2 on aggregate.

After the final whistle I remember a banner being put up by the Wolves fans saying 'you've let us down again'. I didn't understand that because I had never been in that situation before and I was actually really angry anyone should accuse me of letting the club down. But it wasn't aimed at me, I later learned, it was aimed at the club. They had been nearly men for well over a decade now and, although I was the new boy in town, it must have seemed to the supporters that nothing had changed.

After the game I wished Delia all the luck, however they lost the final to Birmingham City on penalties. I still look back at that as a great season in which we played some fantastic football, but in the grand scheme of things it was only the hors d'oeuvre to what was to come in 2002/03.

The following season was always going to be tough because we had at least to match getting to the play-offs. I decided to add only two players to the staff, experienced campaigners Paul Ince and Denis Irwin – but what a difference they made. It still took a few games to get over the massive disappointment of the previous campaign, but after Christmas we went on a run and peaked at the right time to finish fifth.

This time, the play-offs were an entirely different story. We beat Reading home and away in the semi-finals, coming from behind in the first game at Molineux, then hit Sheffield United with everything we had in the final. We could have hammered Manchester United that day, we were that good, at least in the first half when we went in at the break 3-0 ahead. The players were so focussed because of what had happened the previous year. No-one could have beaten us that afternoon.

I remember everyone being on a massive high in the dressing rooms of the Millennium Stadium at half-time, but I said to the players, "You've got two choices. You either go out and carry on entertaining the crowd, or bore the pants off them and make sure we go through 3-0." They asked me which I wanted and I said the latter, so that's what we did. There was no way we were going to let the opportunity slip away of taking this magnificent old football club into the top flight for the first time in a generation. Everyone uses the words 'big club', but other than the first six months I was there, Wolves had virtually full houses every game, two seasons in the Championship and one in the Premiership. Now that's what I call a big club. And the Premiership – football's promised land of riches. I was back where I felt I belonged.

IT WAS NOW three years since the trial had ended, but that seemed irrelevant to a small minority of people who were determined to try to get a rise out of me by chanting my name as a paedophile at football grounds. In the main I had learned to ignore it and concentrate on my job, blocking it all out. But it got to my family, who sat in the stands and had to listen to the abusers spewing forth their filthy bile towards me down on the touchline.

Some supporters think that having a go at the manager has a negative effect on the opposing team. I have always found that logic puzzling. But it does hurt your family, of that have no doubt. I remember playing Ipswich one Christmas. A section of their crowd were singing vile abuse towards me. This was the worst I had ever heard. If they had been singing racist chants they would quite rightly have been thrown out, but chants about what I was meant to have done went unpunished.

That was by no means an isolated incident. It still goes on, even to this day. At Nottingham Forest during the 2008/09 season, I suffered horrible chants for over an hour of the game, yet when I reacted by making a gesture back towards the supporters one of the stewards told me to stop winding up the fans. My daughter Chloe was at the game and I wanted to do something, anything to protect her. Chloe wasn't happy about what I did, but I am not prepared to have my family insulted in this way. Would you be?

Ann:

It seems we can never escape constant reminders of the false accusations against Dave. The season before promotion, Wolves were playing away at Burnley and Chloe and I went along to support Dave. There was a small wall dividing me and the family from several suited men whom I assumed were civilised football fans. They were clearly Burnley supporters being hosted in the directors' guest room.

One of them decided to get up and start giving Dave, who was no more than 12 feet away from us in the dugout, terrible stick, calling him a paedophile and child abuser. Initially I just tried to block it out, but Chloe started crying and saying, "Please mum get him to stop." I kept telling the guy to sit down and keep his mouth shut, but that just made him worse. Some of the things he said were vile.

At half-time, the man was in the same room as me laughing away and drinking his cup of tea. The second half started and off he went again, screaming abuse. He was warned by the Wolves academy director, Chris Evans, in no uncertain terms to shut up, but still took no notice. Then we called a steward over, but to no avail.

"Nothing we can do," he said. Disgraceful.

Midway through the second half an obscenity I can't repeat was hurled in Dave's direction. Chris suddenly leapt to his feet, flew over the wall towards the guy and grabbed him by the neck. He had to be wrestled off this idiot by the stewards who had refused to sort out the situation.

When we came in at full-time I was itching to go over to this idiot and say, 'How dare you talk like that? Dave has been acquitted and he's innocent.' But I was a guest in another club's boardroom, so I left well alone. Eventually the guy left the room, I assumed to go to the toilet. Suddenly Dave walked in and I told him about what had happened. Wouldn't you know, this same guy had only stopped Dave in the corridor outside moments before and asked him for his autograph! The cheek of it. Those are the kind of people we still had to put up with

Dave:

Of all my children affected by the obscene chanting, Chloe was the worst hit. She still is. She hasn't yet developed the kind of immunity to it which I have. I think it's also worse for her, and Ann, because when they come to games, particularly away from home, that is when the abuse can be at its worst and also they are up in the stand right by idiots shouting at me like the guy Ann describes above. I'm apart from it, down in the cauldron and also have my mind focussed on what's happening on the pitch. I tend to block out the crowd naturally anyway, that's how I operate, most managers do.

Having said that, even nearly ten years on from being acquitted, the abuse continues at lots of clubs' grounds – even so-called friendly clubs like Ipswich. At most of them it is only a minority, sometimes even just one or two individuals. I have to wonder why the stewards never intervene? Why these people are never ejected? They are just low-life scum in my opinion.

Even though it's been going on for years and the vast majority of it washes over me, sometimes I do react, even though I shouldn't. It's almost impossible not to. When Leeds were getting relegated from the Championship in 2007 and their fans started chanting the usual crap, I deliberately put my finger downwards as if to say 'you're going down'. I guess you could say that's provocative, but it's hardly the equivalent of screaming filthy and inaccurate abuse at someone. Also I did not do it after just a couple of minutes of being on the receiving end. Oh no, this was after taking their vile abuse for the best part of 80 minutes.

A few days later, I received a letter at the club from this woman, a Leeds fan, who was absolutely disgusted at my antics. The cheek of it. I could just have ignored her, but instead I phoned the woman up and said my piece.

"Excuse me, you are disgusted with my antics?" I said indignantly. "What about all the abuse that I received?"

Her pathetic reply was, "Well it was just football banter."

I replied, "No it wasn't, it's just vile. And the people they are abusing are my children and my wife who have to sit there and listen to it. So think about that. Don't you dare tell me it's football banter."

Then there was an occasion at Stoke – I was manager of Wolves at the time – when I walked out to inspect the pitch before kick-off. The stadium was mostly empty and I was standing by myself judging the surface. Suddenly I heard shouting booming out from the stand, "You f****** pervert, Jones."

I turned around. There was a small group of guys standing together at the front of the main stand, one of whom was staring maniacally at me. I walked towards them. "Who just shouted at me?"

The glances of his mates gave him away.

"Me," he admitted.

"You sad man. Have you got to the ground early and waited here all this time just so you could have a go at me?" I was ready for an argument. "If you have something to say, say it to my face."

His mates knew what he had been shouting. You could see his brain, or what passed for one, whirring, trying to get out of first gear. He stammered, "Er, erm, er."

"Come on," I said. "What have you got to say? Let's hear it."

The veins on his head were pumping as he blurted out, "Jones . . . your coat is crap."

His mates fell about laughing. It was so cold I turned the collar up on my 'crap' coat and walked away from the coward. I still laugh about that insult. And I still have the coat.

HAMSTRUNG BY SIR JACK

WE'D DEVELOPED A three-year plan to win promotion when I joined, and I had achieved it in two. The atmosphere was unbelievable, everyone was pulling the right way. The fans were overwhelmed with joy and swarmed onto the streets of the city to party as we showed off the Play-off final trophy on our open-topped bus tour. Many weren't even born the last time the club were playing the likes of Manchester United and Liverpool back in 1984. They were all deliriously happy.

It was a fantastic achievement, but as we've seen many times before, if you get into the Premiership you have to have funds to strengthen and it is particularly difficult if you are the last club to clinch your place in the top flight by virtue of winning the Play-offs. Fully conversant with what it would take to keep Wolves in the Premier League, soon after winning promotion I went to see Sir Jack and the board to discuss transfer targets. I was looking forward to a decent investment to give us the best chance of establishing ourselves, rather than becoming a yo-yo club who bounces between the top two divisions, too good for one, not good enough for the other. It didn't quite turn out like that.

I was asked three questions. Firstly, how much would I need to keep Wolves in the Premier League?

"Twenty million pounds," I replied.

"How much to finish in the top half?"

"Up to thirty million," was my answer.

"And how much to win the whole thing?"

Amazed as I was by the sheer boldness of the third question, I gave a truthful answer. "Why don't we just consolidate and make sure we stay up, then slowly build?"

At least the questioning seemed to indicate that a significant sum would be coming my way, so imagine my disbelief when the board stumped up next to nothing. Three million quid was all I was offered. Laughable. Peanuts. Pocket money – the kind of investment that buys you one player, and an average one at that. I felt badly let down. One of my daughters was getting married that summer and I might as well have torn up that £3 million and used it as confetti at her wedding for all the good it would do in terms of strengthening the squad. All those 'get me promotion son' promises had come to nothing. My ego and my pride told me that, however unrealistic, I had to stay and attempt to achieve the impossible instead of just walking away, as some would have done.

I had lined up people like England internationals David James, Trevor Sinclair and one or two others who, in total, would have cost around £16 million. None of them were now affordable and I was reduced to bringing in former Tottenham striker Steffen Iverson, Henri Camara, a Senegalese forward from Sedan, and Portuguese midfielder Silas, who didn't work out. We ended up spending £3.5 million.

He never admitted it to me, but I think Sir Jack's parsimony surprised even Jez Moxey. I will never understand why, having waited 19 years to get there, they didn't throw money at it. I never found out Sir Jack's reasons. When we lost our first game 5-1 away at Blackburn, and the second 4-0 at home to Charlton it was obvious we'd got a long, hard fruitless season ahead. To use the expression which famously once me got into trouble for describing a referee's performance, the money the board had given me was 'bobbins'.

In the January transfer window I did get another couple of million, with which I brought in Newcastle forward Carl Cort and Romania striker

Ioan Ganea, but even that was vastly insufficient and anyway we were too far off the pace by then.

The players we had gave everything from day one, but a lot of them knew that, week-in, week-out, they were not of a high enough standard. There were some highs. A particular one I remember was coming back from 3-0 down at half-time to beat Leicester 4-3 thanks to Camara's late goal, but they were few and far between.

At Southampton, I had proved that being in the relegation zone at Christmas didn't necessarily mean going down, but our total of eleven points at the turn of the year was never going to be enough.

I wondered as the season drew towards its inevitable conclusion if I should just walk away. After all my stock was pretty high. Friends and other managers told me I had taken the club as far as I could and that I should move on. I listened, but didn't act. I had a lot of respect for the people at Wolves and even, still, for Sir Jack. I was just confused and angry about how he had failed to back me, the club and the fans following promotion.

LET'S CALL A spade a spade. I didn't enjoy my one season in the Premiership with Wolves one bit, despite having been so desperate to get back there. Week after week my team was getting beaten and there was nothing I could do about it. My hands were tied behind my back. I was having to put teams out who I knew were not capable of getting a result. Plus we lost two of our best players, Joleon Lescott and Matt Murray, through injury for virtually the whole campaign. Joleon didn't kick a single ball in the entire season. His was a massive loss; he had been instrumental in getting the club promoted and was a real up and coming star as he is now proving at Everton. It would have cost millions to replace him. No disrespect to the rest of the players who were all honest and hard-working. They just weren't up to the task; it was soul-destroying for all of us.

Despite some great victories, not least over Manchester United, it was no surprise when we were relegated back down to the Championship, even though if the league had started at Christmas our results would have been good enough to keep us up. It hurt like hell, but I will always believe that if the board had matched my ambitions instead of being so mean-spirited, I would have taken the club on to greater things. Instead, for the first time in my career I had been relegated and we had to start all over again. Not a day went by when it didn't frustrate the life out of me. Once you lose Premiership status, it's incredibly difficult to re-motivate the players. Even though my staff and I were able to switch back into Championship mode, it was always going to take longer for the players and by the time the following Christmas came round, we were only halfway up the table. I honestly believe the team would have got stronger in the second half of the season, but the club had made a decision to get rid of me. Only they can answer this, but I am certain they were listening to outside influences – message boards, things like that. It was crazy because everyone had worked so hard within the restrictions placed on us. Of course we wanted to bounce back straight away, but not a lot of clubs do it. Going up and spending just one season in the Premier League is a very draining experience and the price of failure is all too often a delayed reaction.

I had a fantastic relationship with Sir Jack's son, Rick, who had taken over as chairman. He loved life, but didn't really know anything about football. That only added to an impossible situation.

It all came to a head when we played at Gillingham who were bottom of the table and beat us 1-0. We should have battered them 10-1, but we just could not score and after that the pressure started to grow. Rumours began to fly around and just as we were preparing to travel up to play at Sunderland, I got a call to go and see Rick and Jez. I knew what was coming, you can tell by the tone of voice. I told them I knew what was going on and asked them not to tell the press because my children had gone to school and I wanted to be the one to tell them. Let's face it, my family had some history when it came to the kids finding out about important things before Ann or I had a chance to let them know first.

No chance. On the way in, the news about a summit meeting at Wolves and speculation about my likely departure was all over the radio. Who leaked it? You tell me. Sir Jack had an apartment up in one of the stands and when I walked in, Rick and Jez were pacing up and down.

They asked me if I wanted a cup of tea and Rick said they were going to call it a day.

"I knew this was going to happen," I said.

"How?" asked a surprised Rick.

"Because you didn't give me a saucer with my tea!" I was only cracking a joke, but they were so sensitive about it all they actually went and got me one.

I honestly don't think Rick wanted to sack me, I think it was down to his father. Time is a precious commodity in football, nobody ever gives you enough. Nobody sticks with people any more. It seems to be a constant battle – managers want more of it, chairmen and owners are prepared to give less and less.

You could argue that Wolves were not progressing because we had been relegated, but I believe this wasn't the case. The only reason we had been relegated was because the board didn't back me. They had made their decision after winning promotion and now I was paying for it. And to make things worse they went and employed my stalker. That's right, Glenn Hoddle. Again.

I think they originally wanted to give Stuart Gray a go at it. Stuart was on my coaching staff just as he had been at Southampton. Initially he became caretaker after they sacked me, but his results didn't stack up in the month or so he was in charge, and anyway I think the board had their heads turned by Hoddle's 'name'. He is, after all, a former England, Tottenham and Chelsea manager.

You could say my time at Molineux ended in tears, but that's invariably what happens with most managers at most clubs. I've always believed, whenever I've gone into any football club, do it correctly, treat people properly. I felt I had done that at Wolves and I expected that back in return. After some wrangling, I did receive everything that I was owed. Chairmen always seem to thank managers publicly for the work they have done, but behind the scenes so many of them play hardball when it comes to paying up. I don't bear any grudges over things like that. It got sorted and we have all moved on.

A few weeks after I was sacked, I was covering a Sky game, Leeds versus Wolves, and I bumped into Sir Jack and Jez as they were leaving

Elland Road. We shook hands and I wished them all the best. That was that.

I'm genuinely pleased to see Wolves have got back to the top flight under Mick McCarthy, but it is essential Mick is given sufficient backing now they have reached the Premier League again. I'm sure he will. I hope he does. I was delighted to hear Jez Moxey state shortly after Wolves had clinched the 2008/09 Championship title that they will not make the same mistake as last time.

IT WAS CHRISTMAS again and I was out of work, which always seemed to happen to me. Luckily there wasn't that much disruption on the domestic front. Chloe was at university, Danielle was living in Southampton and Lea in Southport. We would only have to move Georgia out of school, but not until I had found work somewhere else. This time, I took a nice break, went on a few holidays, went back to my golf and my gardening. I took full advantage of this chance to spent quality time with the family. As all football managers will tell you, you don't get a great deal of that. All the time you are doing something, going somewhere, watching games, watching players. It's a 24/7 job. People from outside the game don't see that side of your life. They think you just turn up on a match day. I used the next five months or so to put some real family bonding in place. I also did a lot of charity stuff as I waited for the next move. I had a decent enough reputation and thought it wouldn't be long before someone else came in for me. My record was pretty good, the relegation on my CV being the only blip, but down to a particular set of circumstances that were well known in the game. Thankfully I was right.

My first contact with Cardiff City came through an agent acting for Sam Hammam and Peter Ridsdale. They wanted to meet me in London at the Landmark Hotel. I had already been touted for the QPR job as Ian Holloway was on gardening leave, but from my standpoint they had a manager still in contract and, after all I had been through, I felt it was unethical to talk to them as a result. I knew both Sam and Peter from their time at Wimbledon and Leeds respectively. Peter's somewhat tarnished reputation from his Leeds days didn't even enter my head as

I drove down to London in May for the interview. I had no pre-conceived ideas. I simply didn't know what to expect.

SAM THE MAN

CARDIFF HAD JUST managed to avoid relegation at the end of the 2004/05 season and had asked Lenny Lawrence to step down. Peter and Sam outlined what plans they had for the club, but they had a slight problem. They had no money. I asked how they could possibly have plans with no money. I didn't get an entirely satisfactory answer, but within hours of the interview, Peter called me and offered me the job. I accepted and went home to Wolverhampton with Sam's request not to tell anyone ringing in my ears. As so often happens, however, someone had leaked it and my appointment was all over the following day's papers. Cue a highly displeased Sam calling me up and asking me who I had told. "Nobody," I replied before adding, "but without being funny, to interview me in the foyer of the Landmark Hotel when people are walking around saying hello to me, is it really surprising news has got out?"

As it turned out, there was an agent in the same foyer having a drink with one if his players. I won't name either of them, but it was that agent who spotted me and called the press. That's the trouble with agents, you just don't know where they will turn up.

I took the job on the basis that if I did well early on I'd have my contract re-negotiated. The first year I wasn't on fantastic money, but I was prepared to show them what I could do and if they were happy we would continue together. I negotiated this agreement with Peter, who was chief executive at the time, but when he told Sam the details immediate complications developed. I went down to Sam's house to sign the deal and meet his wife and fantastic family, really lovely people. Peter was already there, complete with champagne to celebrate. Out of the blue, at the very last minute, Sam decided to change the goalposts and offer me more money. Peter, who was just about to pop the cork in celebration, panicked. The cork came out alright, but the champagne went everywhere except the glasses. Having spent all day taking him through the fine detail he was incredulous at what Sam had done. He had ripped up hours of hard work and negotiation which we'd both been happy with. In the end I signed for what I had agreed with Peter after the pair of them went off and had a few words, but that was Sam all over. He was a free spirit who at times just didn't think things through properly.

The first thing I did was call up Terry Burton whom I had met on various coaching courses. He was already at Cardiff and I wanted to have the run-down on the players since pre-season was just around the corner. I drove down to have dinner with Terry, Sam and Peter in a local restaurant. When I got there, I was told they had to sell players to survive. I said, "Okay go ahead, sell what you have to sell and tell me when the business is done. Then I'll know what players we need to bring in."

I told Sam I was going away on a fortnight's holiday to America and he wasn't happy at all with that. I couldn't see what the problem was. All managers take vacations in the summer and anyway I would be on the end of a phone and a fax even in the States. What would I do being in Cardiff sitting in an office in June while they sold players around me? It all got a bit fraught and Peter told me privately that Sam thought they had made a mistake, that because of my holiday plans they shouldn't have appointed me. Sam had expected me to turn up for work straight away. Peter told Sam that was a silly attitude, that I was just behaving like every other manager and that it wasn't right to expect me to cancel.

When I returned, refreshed and invigorated for pre-season, frankly I nearly died. I simply couldn't believe the state of the club. They had no training facilities to speak of, no infrastructure, nothing. The first priority was to try and find a training base we could use throughout the season. The one they had been using on a temporary basis was nicknamed 'Dog shit park' because it was just that: a local park where all the dogs did their business when they were taken for walks. The club had arranged to go to Scotland for a pre-season tour. As I got on the bus, it felt and smelt pretty musty. I honestly thought I was going back 25 years. What on earth had I let myself in for? I looked at the players getting into the bus after me: a load of kids, not a team as such. So no money, no players and debt-ridden. In my haste to get a job at a Championship club had I made a huge mistake myself?

To say it was a culture shock was an understatement. Not surprisingly, the criterion for my first season was simply survival in the Championship, but even that was clearly going to be an unenviable challenge. Terry and the staff – good people, good coaches – sat down with me and drew up a plan. We needed to get people in, and quick, to do a short-term job. Before we could put anything into practice, though, we had this wretched Scotland trip to contend with which hardly got off to the best of starts when we learned we couldn't use the training ground we had earmarked near our hotel because a young apprentice had died tragically by being electrocuted. It had to be shut down, and rightly so.

Somehow we got through it and, by the time the season proper got under way, we had made improvements to the playing staff. Ann and I had decided we would sell our house in Shropshire and move back down to the Southampton area and I would commute to Cardiff. We wanted to be nearer to Danielle and loved Hampshire. We looked at a few houses, didn't find anything and I decided to have a look round Cardiff on my own after training each day. I quickly realised what people saw in the place. I had this vision of Cardiff being mines and steel factories, run down and old. It was the complete opposite: a fantastic city, regenerated, effervescent, surrounded by valleys and beaches. Ann came and stayed in a hotel with me for a month and fell in love with the place. We got an apartment down near the bay which was fantastic for the city and its vibrant nightlife, but realistically we needed somewhere bigger because of the dogs and rented a house before eventually buying our own place in a tiny village a few miles outside the city.

I had read a lot of things about Sam Hammam and what a control freak he was, but I had thought much of it was hype until I worked for him. He insisted on being in the dug-out and in the dressing room; he used to ask what my dream team was, even though there was no chance of ever getting it. He loved to play with names, dangling them tantalisingly in front of me as if we had some chance of signing players like Michael Owen and Frank Lampard. It was ridiculous and I couldn't work that way. For me it's all about getting the job done with the resources available and being judged fairly on that.

I will always remember having a meeting about what players we were going to target to bring in. My staff and I brainstormed a list of targets we could conceivably attract. We gave the list of names to Sam.

"No, no, no, they're not good enough," he said.

We asked who he'd like, then.

"Why don't we try and get Steed Malbranque from Fulham," he replied. I knew Malbranque wanted out of Fulham – he eventually went to Spurs – but what on earth possessed Sam to imagine the guy would join Cardiff? I considered the conversation I would have to have with Chris Coleman, then manager of Fulham. I'd phone him and ask whether we could have Malbranque on loan and pay him £3,000 a week in wages when he was on something like 40 grand. Oh and by the way, you pay the difference!

Can you imagine what Chris would have said? He'd have thought I'd gone absolutely mad which is exactly what I thought of Sam. I told him there was no way I was making that phone call. He said I had to think big, but there was no point in that unless we had the finances to back it up.

I said we should chase players we could afford and who I knew would do a good job for the club. Sam then decided he wanted us to write down three teams: the one we had already, the one we thought we could get and the ultimate dream team. I wasn't into playing those sort of games. It was a case of getting our heads down and building. Sam, being the ultimate self-publicist, had visions that would never be fulfilled in a million years. They were fantasies. I wouldn't say we argued, but we were definitely not on the same wavelength. It was certainly a frustrating and difficult relationship. Not the kind you really want with your employer.

On the other hand Peter Ridsdale was fantastic. He would constantly tell me what we could afford, only for Sam to stick his oar in and say who he wanted to go for instead, even though it was patently obvious we didn't have a cat in hell's chance. In the art of self-delusion, Sam was up there with the biggest practitioners.

These were hardly the ideal circumstances in which to manage, but I was determined to give it my best shot. In the end, we worked it so that I would target the players, and Peter would go and tell Sam what we were doing. It developed into a great double act. I struck up an instant rapport with Peter from day one. He may not be everyone's cup of tea, but he kept me informed of everything. It's not that I didn't like Sam, on the contrary I did. It's just that he became an obstruction as far as running the club was concerned. Sam was fabulous company and a huge personality who had the success of Cardiff City at heart. He just couldn't see the wood for the trees most of the time.

You might be wondering by now why I took the job in the first place. Number one I thought it was a challenge and number two I knew it was the sort of club I could help grow and which had a fantastic fan base. I was buying into their potential. What I had no idea of was just how close to the bone the coffers of the club were. It's not uncommon for managers to have restricted budgets to work with, and in fact that had been the case for me throughout my career, but the Cardiff cupboard was pretty much bare.

Many people felt that Sam was responsible for the club almost hitting the skids in a very public way over the next couple of years. I was never involved on the financial side, but it was hard not to be aware of what was going on the day Cardiff almost went under. We were travelling up to a game at Coventry, and things were so desperate that we didn't know whether the game would go ahead or whether the club would be wound up and we would be turning round and going back down the motorway. I was on tenterhooks, but trying hard not to let it show as if the players got wind that this was the day of reckoning the chances were they'd stop the bus and get off. At best if the game went ahead I needed to get a performance out of them which was not affected by them all thinking about where their next wage packet was coming from.

At around 11.45am, just fifteen minutes before the midday deadline, Peter rang me to say that it had all been sorted and the game could go ahead. It was a huge relief. I returned that night and rang Peter to find out exactly what had gone on and learned that the club had been taken over and he was now Chairman. I was very pleased about that, although having said that, it was a sad day as Sam was leaving. He had become a Cardiff legend and had begun the process of stirring a club which had been wasting away over the previous decade into action.

As Sam said his goodbyes I felt as sick to the stomach as I had all those years before when Danny Bergara cleared out his office at Stockport. It's hard to explain, but when someone parts company with something they love, you have to be really cold-hearted not to sympathise. We all know, though, that Sam had to go. The club would never ever have moved on had he stayed. We'd have worried every month about if the wages were going to be paid and it could have got very messy. I had been told that none of the banks wanted to deal with the club. Wherever Sam is now, he'll know what I'm talking about, but no-one can take away the good things he did for Cardiff City.

UP FOR THE CUP

WHEREVER I GO and whatever I do for the rest of my career in football, Wembley 2008 will always stand out as one of the most thrilling moments of my life. Call me a traditionalist, but I still believe the FA Cup is the greatest cup competition in the world. Most managers and players never even get near to the final. It is my proudest achievement in football that I took an unfashionable, under-resourced club such as Cardiff City all the way to the final.

There were some pretty tricky hurdles to negotiate on the way, though. We were having a better than average, but not earth-shattering, season, but expectations were nevertheless high, as they always are. As far as Cardiff fans are concerned, we are the Manchester United of south Wales. Sometimes the expectations are unrealistic, but over the last two years the dream has started to become a reality in terms of how far we have come.

Perhaps those dreams had been fuelled by the growing ambition we were showing as a club. We had taken the decision to make two very high profile signings in the close season, Jimmy Floyd Hasselbaink and Robbie Fowler. Both were strikers who were coming to the end of their careers and who had had their fair share of injury problems, but how lucky we were to get them. I bumped into Robbie in a restaurant out in Orlando, where he has a house. Ann, myself and the girls had gone for a meal and met him by chance. I asked what he was doing and he said he was thinking about maybe going over to Australia to play, though nothing definite had been agreed. I sat chatting to him for about 20 minutes telling him about all the hard work we were putting into Cardiff.

A couple of weeks after I returned to England, I was at a golf tournament at Celtic Manor and Robbie was playing in it too. I got chatting to him again and asked him whether he'd consider coming to Cardiff. He said he had other options, so I suggested he had a chat with the chairman since they knew each other from their time at Leeds United. We never thought we'd have a chance of signing him. The problem when we did was that we had to get him fit. We pushed and pushed, but probably ended up making the hip problem he'd carried for some time worse. Having said that, the reaction to signing him really put Cardiff City on the map. It propelled the club into a new light. Now supporters and players could see that we could attract players of that calibre. What I didn't tell Robbie was that we didn't have a training ground to speak of, that Ninian was old and run down. I sold him the dream, but when he arrived, he said that if he'd have known what he was coming to, he probably wouldn't have signed. It was slightly tongue-in-cheek, but he was a lovely lad. It's just so unfortunate that the fans only saw him strut his stuff on a few occasions.

As for Jimmy, he was on his way to Leicester, but I think he'd had a few problems with someone at the club, so we nipped in and signed him. I took him down to a hotel and again sold him the dream of the new stadium and what we were trying to achieve. I said we needed people of his calibre to try and move on to the next stage. He came in with this big reputation and a lot of people tried to put me off him, but I'd managed people like this before so I wasn't scared at the prospect at all. In fact I like that kind of challenge. Unfortunately for Jimmy and the chairman, they'd agreed on something verbally but both parties interpreted it differently. It eventually went to a tribunal and was sorted out at the end of the season. It was a sad way to end. I have no regrets at all in signing him. Both Jimmy and Robbie brought something to the club that we had never seen before.

Back to the cup run and in the third round we drew non-league Chase-town, who were appearing at this stage of the competition for the very first time having beaten Port Vale. This was their cup final. They were actually the lowest positioned club in the history of the competition to get that far as they were in the British Gas Business Southern League Midlands Division One and there were six divisions and 136 league places separating us. Charlie Blakemore, their manager, was a staunch Wolves supporter who said some nice things about me from my time there. Yet here we were with everything to lose and nothing to gain in what was the biggest game in Chasetown's history. We took them seriously enough to send scouts to look at the players and the pitch. The report we got back was that the latter was an absolute bog. We like to try and play football so it didn't augur too well. Chasetown had the chance to move the tie, after all they would be invaded by legions of Cardiff fans if they staged it at their tiny ground. I think privately the authorities would have loved them to take up the offer to avoid any trouble, but I could understand it when they didn't.

The weather had been pretty awful in the days leading up to the game so we made a decision with their chairman that we would help them to get the game on. It had been selected for live TV coverage, so it benefited both of us for it to go ahead as we would most likely lose the TV money if it was postponed. Our groundsman assisted in preparing the surface and sorting out the drainage while we also gave them some advice on hospitality etc. Mind you with comedian Frank Carson on their board of directors they didn't really need much helping on the hosting and banter side of things.

It was a huge day for the Staffordshire club and the tiny ground was packed with 2,420 fervent supporters who went absolutely ballistic when, in the 17th minute, our full-back Kevin McNaughton, turned a swirling cross past our goalkeeper. I couldn't believe it. We were so much in control it was untrue, but the goal gave Chasetown the impetus. I think reporters and commentators alike were rehearsing their fairytale lines, until we equalised in injury time at the end of the first half through Peter Whittingham. That goal changed the game and we won comfortably in the end thanks to a debut goal from 17-year-old wonderkid Aaron Ramsey, who we would shortly sell to Arsenal for £5 million, and another of our superb youngsters, Paul Parry, who netted the clinching third.

After the game I was fulsome in my praise for what our opponents had achieved. I knew how hard it was for them to simply exist and that this day had really been all about them. Chasetown did everything the right way. They treated us with respect and a lot of appreciation. After the game – and I've never seen anything like this before – their players came into our dressing room to ask for our players' shirts. They took just about everything: shirts, shorts, socks, boots, ties, any mementos they could lay their hands on. We were happy to oblige because of the way we had been received. They even presented us with a trophy and put up a big marquee for a party afterwards. We were lucky to get out of that ground wearing anything at all!

We built up such a strong relationship with Chasetown that it was agreed they would play one of the warm-up games when we move into our new stadium. Clubs like Chasetown are what the romance of the FA Cup is all about. I firmly believe in that romance. It was partly that which gave us the belief to go on that run to the new Wembley.

The next round, Hereford away, could not have been more different. We pulled into their car park and wound the window down and it was a case of 'who are you?' and 'we can't be bothered'. Perhaps it was because they were a league club that they showed us scant respect. But we got the result we needed, winning 2-1.

Then came the fifth round and what a draw, Wolves at home. You could hardly have written a more poignant script for me personally. Regardless of my past association with the club, I tried to treat it as just another game. We got off to a fantastic start and won 2-0 with a pair of cracking goals from Jimmy Floyd Hasselbaink and Peter Whittingham. I don't think my replacement at Wolves Mick McCarthy would argue with the fact that we deserved it.

Now we were in the quarter-final and I did begin to wonder to myself, could this possibly be our year? Especially that season as the big teams were dropping like flies. Barnsley had just beaten Liverpool at Anfield, while Arsenal had been knocked out at Manchester United.

We certainly got a sense of something, though not many neutrals shared that view when the draw took us to Middlesbrough who were struggling but were nevertheless a Premier League club. We had just started to hit form and arrived at the Riverside full of confidence. I remember overhearing one of the stewards talking about how much he was looking forward to going to Wembley for the semi-finals. According to him, it was all done and dusted. Well we went out and played absolutely brilliantly, played them off the park in fact. It was our best performance by far in the competition. We showed no fear and got a lot of plaudits after early goals by Peter Whittingham and Roger Johnson won us the game 2-0.

That result was a springboard for people outside Cardiff to suddenly get interested in us, to come and see what our long-term plans were and how we were not just some club who had struck lucky in the cup and had no other ambition.

Now things really began to spiral. When Barnsley upset Chelsea at the same stage, all of a sudden there was a Championship dominance of the semi-finals — three clubs from our division, and only one, Portsmouth, who had knocked out Manchester United at Old Trafford, from the Premier League. I remember all the local press being at what, by now, was our spanking new training ground at the Vale of Glamorgan for the semi-final draw which we watched on TV together. The staff were happily playing head tennis when it was announced that we were to play Barnsley. The place went ballistic, phones ringing off the hook. We'd got the best draw possible and had an excellent chance of reaching the final. All eyes were on us as we prepared for the club's biggest day for years.

Some people aren't happy when semi-finals are at Wembley, arguing that the stadium is a special place and should only hold finals. I don't subscribe to that. The people who say that are those who regularly get to finals. For the four semi-finalists that year, it was a major achievement to get that far, so why rob us of the chance to play there when two of us wouldn't get another one, perhaps for a lifetime? It wasn't as if the stadium was half-full. We sold our entire ticket allocation and so did Barnsley. I just knew we were going to win. We'd beaten them away in the league and I knew we were a better and stronger team. It was just whether the nerves would hold out. It all went to plan, though. Joe Ledley, another of our great youngsters, scored early on with an outstanding left-foot volley and we had some other chances to kill it before they came more and more into the game. When their big striker Kayode Odejayi, who had been the hero of their victory over Chelsea, missed a crucial one-on-one with our keeper, I knew it would be our day. Cardiff City in the FA Cup final. Talk about breaking the mould.

In the league we were still in with a shout of getting to the play-offs, but the cup run killed that off. We had to beat relegation-threatened Scunthorpe away to stand any chance and we led 1-0 at half-time, only for them to come out for the second half and really set about us. It's probably the only time I've ever seen my Cardiff team be bullied and kicked out of a game. I could see some of my players not going into tackles for fear of getting injured. Some of them were a trifle half-hearted. I didn't like it, but I could understand it. You can't get away from the fact that they were thinking about the Cup final. Nobody wanted to miss out. We lost 3-2 and I feel we did lose our way because the Cup final had a major bearing on our performances late on.

As fate would have it our final league game immediately before the final was against Barnsley at Ninian Park. We absolutely pulverised them. For that game the reverse psychology was in operation. Everyone wanted to make sure they got the shirt for Wembley.

We travelled down to London on a special train the day before the final to try and replicate what the 1927 Cardiff team, which was the only side ever to take the FA Cup out of England when they beat Arsenal in the final, had done. Because we knew there would be thousands going from Cardiff on the motorway, we didn't want to get stuck in traffic. When we got to Cardiff station, thousands of fans were there to see us off, the carriages bedecked in blue and white. We stayed at the Landmark Hotel, just as we had for the semi-final. The atmosphere was pretty relaxed and low-key. Nobody said too much. Everyone had the final on their minds.

We certainly had some characters in the dressing room, none more so than Jimmy Floyd Hasselbaink who had been talked up beforehand as our most likely match-winner. I liked Jimmy, had a lot of time for him. People talk about player power and how Jimmy was a rough diamond, but it's a load of rubbish. If the chairman thinks a player is above the manager, then yes you can have a problem but that has never been the case with me. I had a good relationship with Jimmy. Perhaps it got a bit sour at the end when there was a difference of opinion between him and Peter about a new contract at the end of the season, but there are no hard feelings. We also, of course, had Robbie Fowler who wasn't fit enough to play in the final. Robbie was a likeable guy, but his hip injury meant he couldn't get back to the levels of fitness that were needed. Perhaps we tried to get him fit quicker than we should have done.

At the final itself, the Pompey fans refrained from giving me any serious stick which I am grateful for, apart from the odd 'Cheer up Davy Jones' chant which I could accept, as it was only to do with my involvement with Southampton and nothing to do with the court case. It was a very good-natured game and Harry actually said when he went to pick the trophy up that it felt like an old-fashioned final because the beaten supporters stayed on to cheer both teams. I had been to see Manchester United play Chelsea in the final the previous year and by the time Chelsea collected the trophy the United fans had vacated the stadium. It was half empty. This time Wembley stayed full. Maybe it was because both sets of fans wanted to milk the atmosphere right to the end. This was a special, one-off day out for everyone concerned. It was a wonderful occasion.

I felt we had been a bit unlucky. We had a couple of good chances but to be fair, we needed to score first and have the Premier League side chase us rather than the other way round. Once Kanu netted from close in just before half-time we were going to have problems breaking them down. But we gave it a good go. Harry showed us a lot of respect by playing five across the middle of the pitch to stifle our creative midfield. He was frightened that if we played to our potential and they were off their game, we could beat them. The sad thing is that we went home without the trophy, but the occasion itself was the stuff of dreams. My whole family were there; Ann, the kids, my brothers and sister, aunties, uncles. My seven-year-old grandson walked out onto the pitch with me, which was wonderful. But the most thrilling thing of all was having my mum there. Dad would have been so proud.

The Cup final was the moment when I felt I had achieved enough to fulfil my burning ambition. I knew in my heart that somewhere Dad was with me. I wouldn't say reaching Wembley helped me get my life back on track because I had already won promotion to the Premiership with Wolves. What it did do was achieve something that few other managers have on their CV. I'd played in a League Cup final, but this was the Cup final that was beamed across the world, a showpiece. It somehow felt like the end of a journey. My belief was restored the day I got back into management, but to reach that Cup final was my dream, the next best thing after getting there as a player.

Cup final day is a huge family occasion. You can't really express the magnitude of it in words for both sides of the family and how much having everyone there meant to me.

AFTERWARDS, EVERYONE WAS bussed from the stadium to the Chelsea Harbour Hotel where all the wives had been staying and we had a huge party. It didn't matter that we'd lost, the place was buzzing. Together we had achieved something no Cardiff side had for 80 years. That's another of the things I love about the FA Cup. It creates new and unlikely heroes. Glen Loovens, Tony Capaldi, Stephen McPhail, Paul Parry and Gavin Rae are hardly household names, but gained some degree of recognition only because of the Cup.

The Cup final may not have the same aura or standing in some quarters of this country as it used to, but let me tell you something, when we went on our pre-season programme a few weeks later, we were not billed as Cardiff City but as FA Cup finalists. That's the kind of reputation the competition still has globally. We had been propelled into a different league. It was an unbelievable achievement.

One Premier League manager let himself down by saying it was a fluke to have such a strong Championship presence in the last four. You can surely only beat the teams the draw places in front of you. It was not our fault that the big teams had failed and gone out. Anyway, on the way we had knocked out Middlesbrough who had beaten Chelsea in the league. I know football doesn't work like that, but we still had to win five games to get to the final. Is that a fluke? I don't think so.

Also, the timing was perfect for us as a club on the up. We had just opened the new training ground, one of the best outside the Premier League, and with the new stadium set to open before the start of 2009/10 season, you couldn't have asked for a better start to what everyone at Cardiff is describing as a new era after generations of under-achieving. Look at the players we have now, even though we have had to sell some of our best young talent as does any club in the Championship, the quality of our squad is second to none. We are now a very attractive proposition for any player, and that's all down to hard work behind the scenes. The last 18 months have transformed Cardiff City football club. The Bluebirds are flying high again . . . the dawn of a new club, almost.

ONE GOAL FROM GLORY

SINCE I HAVE been at Cardiff, myself and Peter Ridsdale have earned the club over £25m in player sales. Despite this, when we started the 2008/09 season following the euphoria of the Cup final, I felt we had enough ability to compete for promotion to the Premier League.

Peter and I spoke at the start of the season about carrying on where we had left off, even though some of the players had left including Hasselbaink, Fowler, Glen Loovens and, of course, Aaron Ramsey, who we'd sold to Arsenal. Throughout August we were fighting to keep hold of Joe Ledley, who was being pursued by a couple of top-flight clubs, whilst at the same time trying to get players in. The feeling around the training ground was that if we could get into the play-offs it would constitute an excellent season in terms of progress. I think at that stage a 7th placed finish would have been acceptable, however the way things turned out it was far from it.

How did it happen? How could we have been in the top six for virtually 42 games, but take one point out of our last 12 and miss the play-offs not even on goal difference but by having scored a single goal less than Preston? That's the question Cardiff fans and most neutrals are probably still asking themselves. They're not the only ones. I've asked myself the same thing a million times. Let me try to answer as honestly as I can. Ultimately I have to admit we just didn't have enough about us to take us that extra yard. In my opinion, it was lack of experience coupled with nerves. It certainly had nothing to do with ability because for 42 games we were outstanding. Maybe in the last four games it all caught up with the players: we had played a lot of games in a short space of time because we'd got behind in the league after going so far in the Cup again. As we played catch-up the nerves and the tension got to some of them. You always have that small doubt, but in the heat of battle you put it to the back of your mind. I was pretty sure I had the squad to get us into the play-offs if not the top two to earn automatic promotion, but football has a tendency to kick you in the teeth. One minute an FA Cup final, the next the agony of missing out by one goal. What I can say for sure is that what happened to us will take a long time to work its way out of my system. Until, in fact, I can go one step further.

I can't begin to describe the contrast in my mood compared with 12 months earlier. I was lower than a snake's belly. I just hope we'll all get stronger as result of it. I'm sure we will. In fact I will ensure we do.

There is no doubt that the 6-0 drubbing we received that dreadful afternoon at Preston a few weeks before the end of the season hurt us, and hurt us badly. If we'd have lost even 5-0 we'd have made the play-offs instead of them, and then who knows what might have happened? Of course we didn't know that at the time, you just never know in a season which game will be the pivotal one. But that was the result that will haunt us until we can wash the memory away.

Having said that, we all felt confident of getting something at Hills-borough in that ultimately fateful final fixture. The players had been very relaxed and competitive in training and in the first half against Wednesday, who were mid-table, we had enough chances to get our noses in front including hitting the post with a header. I'd left top scorer Ross McCormack on the bench and went with Chopra up front. I felt the team I put out should have been good enough to get the required result. At half-time we were a bit down not to be ahead and the results else-where affected the team more than we had anticipated. I impressed upon the players that we still had our foot in the door, that we still had that point we needed. But once Wednesday scored with a wonderful goal I could see the belief drain out of them. They were shaken to the core.

It got worse when Wednesday flashed Preston's 2-1 scoreline up on the big screen and the home fans started chanting, "You're not going up". That was hard on the players and I felt for them. I don't believe putting up the score, with the psychological pressure that obviously ensued, was the right thing to do. Why didn't they do the same thing when it was 1-1?

At the final whistle I can't describe the sheer anguish that ripped through me. It was a dreadful, hollow feeling. I received loads of supportive texts and emails saying how sorry everyone was, even from journalists and supporters! How some of them got hold of my mobile number, God only knows. To miss out by one goal was horrifying but it wasn't just down to that one game, it was the last four.

My immediate reaction to the failure to make the play-offs was to tell the players in the dressing room at Hillsborough that changes would need to be made because we hadn't been able to see it through. They'd had it within their grasp, but when the pressure really piled on maybe some of them couldn't deal with it.

It was a horrible journey home. No-one spoke on the coach. The staff felt really let down. Ann was driving behind us with the family, all of whom were in an emotional state, just like I was, but if ever football needed putting in perspective it came on the way home. There was an accident on the motorway. It looked nasty and we stopped the coach and offered our services because we had doctors on board. They weren't required and thankfully no-one had been killed.

When I eventually got home, I looked under my car to see whether I had run over a black cat, wondering why everything had all turned against us. I slept in fits and starts as I tried to figure out what, if anything, I had done wrong. When I got up the next morning Ann and I took the dogs down to the beach for a walk, to try and clear the air a bit and get some wind through my ears. It helped. There is no point in moping around feeling sorry for yourself no matter how intense the disappointment. It was the biggest setback I have suffered as a football manager and that includes going down with Wolves. The important thing is how you respond to such kicks in the teeth and that you do it as a team.

Ann:

That final afternoon of the season we were all in bits, but it was especially bad for me. For some reason I had imagined that Preston had to win by two clear goals to pip us for the play-offs. Because their score was 2-1, I thought we had done it, so as soon as the final whistle went, I flew downstairs to watch Sky in the lounge. Unbeknown to me, the rest of the family and all the wives thought I had run out because I was crying – which is exactly what I did when I saw the pictures on TV of the Preston players celebrating on the pitch. It was a double blow. I thought we'd done it, but I had worked it out wrong.

Everyone was completely devastated, even more so than when we didn't make it up with Wolves. This time it seemed so unfair; we'd been in pole position for most of the season.

When Dave arrived home we just gave each other a long hug as if to say 'we're together in this'. That night the house felt so silent. I can't compare it to a bereavement, but there is a constant ache inside. This is my husband's career, the family's lifestyle, our future. It goes deeper than supporting the club. I started worrying about what the board might do, a feeling that will probably stay with me until Dave can repair things. I'd be lying if I said the summer won't have a tinge of regret overshadowing it.

Dave:

I spoke to each of the players individually as I set about identifying those who hadn't been able to hold their nerve, sifting through the debris and seeing where we could put things right. The task now is to strike a delicate balancing act between those who I feel will learn from it and come back better equipped after the summer, and those who will have to leave.

Everyone inside the club was shell-shocked. I accept there were a lot of very annoyed people and, of course, I looked at myself as well as the players. Did I pick the right team? Did I get this right, did I get that right? We take collective responsibility, that's the way I have always been. I can't put the blame on any one player. So why, you might ask, will I have to change things? Because that's what managers are paid to do. I may have shouldered some of the blame, but I'm not out there playing. I have to find the answers and they probably lie in some new personnel.

I also have to say that some of the reaction in the local press has been over the top. The Cardiff Blues rugby team lost in a semi-final the same weekend we missed out on the play-offs. The rugby team were gutted, according to the local press, while we were gutless. All season long the players had co-operated and had had nice things written about them as a result. Now all of a sudden they were gutless. When I start my press conferences again after the summer, I'm going to make it clear that nobody calls me gutless. Or my team. I tried at times during the season to be reasonable, to pull one or two of the reporters aside and discuss ways we could improve relations. I know they have a job to do, but when we lost to Swansea in the Carling Cup they character assassinated every one of my players. That was our first loss for 17 games, including pre-season and 12 league fixtures. I warned them at the time that we don't mind being criticised for losing, but their reaction was over the top. They seem to have lost sight of the fact that the expectations at Cardiff City football club have grown for one reason and one reason alone: the sheer hard work and determination of me, my staff, the chairman and the players. We have come one hell of a long way. It is just not yet far enough.

It's pretty much exactly the same scenario as what happened to me at Wolves. In the season we thought we'd go up, we didn't. The following year we became stronger and finally made it. I know some people will say Cardiff are a different case, that we blew it and won't get as good a chance again since this division is notoriously hard to get out of. But why shouldn't we? Wolves have just done it haven't they? They finished just outside the play-offs last time around and have now gone up automatically. And good luck to Mick. Everyone was calling for his head at one point, just as some sections have done for mine. Okay we should have been there instead of Preston, but look how many times Preston

o the play-offs. They had just that little bit more experience.
e, done it. We hadn't. It was new territory to my squad. And
let's nᵤ forget that Preston ended up being beaten by Sheffield United
in the play-off semi-final.

None of this is an excuse. People say what happened to us was fate.
That had nothing to do with it. We just stopped doing what we'd been
doing for 42 games, and that isn't acceptable. We'd had one of the best
defensive records all season and scored a lot of goals. Suddenly in four
games, it just dried up. That's not ability. That's nerves, that's know-
how, or lack of it. It tells you something about your players. The only
way to gain that knowledge is to channel all the anger and hurt and use
all that energy to achieve success the following year – which is exactly
what I am intending to do.

However hurt people are – and no-one is hurting more than me – you
cannot deny the club has made huge strides in the last 18 months.
Maybe that's why my chairman said such nice things about me and told
the world that I was going nowhere in the aftermath of failure. Peter
knows that I had made mistakes, but had done more things right than
wrong and I'd like to think that in the cold light of day most would agree
with those sentiments.

When I sat down with the chairman to analyse what had happened,
Peter asked me whether my staff were good enough. I told him that if
they were for 42 games, they don't suddenly become poor just because
of four matches. Yes we could have done better – far better – but it was
still an achievement in itself, the club's best league finish since relegation from top flight in 1928/29. That's why Cardiff have kept faith with
me instead of washing it all away, as so many clubs make the mistake of
doing. Words like 'get rid' and 'sack' are just kneejerk reactions. You have
to look at the bigger picture. Look how far we have come, not only on
the pitch but in terms of the new training facilities and new stadium
which opens with a friendly against our friends from Chasetown and
then the first official fixture against Celtic on 22 July 2009.

When the stadium opens I'm sure the excitement level will grow.
Then it's up to us as a group to make sure we get things right. It's going
to be hard but this has been the first year I've been able to work with

only one rather than both hands tied behind my back. That's why we mustn't lose sight of our ultimate ambition. You can mope around thinking about what might have been, but I will put that behind me and crack on.

When the new season starts I will bring up the pain of losing out by that single goal over the course of the season all the time. I won't stop reminding the players how it feels. Not because I want to punish them, but because I don't want them to ever forget it, I don't want them to think that any single second of a season does not count. The margins are so small in football that you have to keep your foot on the gas all the time. I want the players to use it as a positive, an experience they have had to go through to ultimately become successful. We have to make it happen next time. It's not going to be easy because of the teams coming down from the Premiership – Newcastle, West Brom and Middlesbrough, who will all be desperate to return to the top flight at the first time of asking – but we'll be ready to meet the challenge head on. That is all I have done through my career, throughout my life.

Ann:

It's going to take a long time for the family to get over the bitter disappointment of this season. Dave will only be happy when he fulfils his ultimate ambition of getting back to the Premier League. Whether the abuse he occasionally still gets will be a thing of the past by then, I don't know. Danielle and I even heard it on the car radio once as we were listening to a Cardiff away game live. Just as we were about to switch it off, being able to take no more of the foul chants being directed towards David from a section of the home fans, the welsh commentator told listeners, "this is absolutely appalling and it needs to be stamped out." Maybe now that people have read how it affected me, Dave and the family, it will. A decade ago, my husband faced going to prison for 17 years. I might have had to face life without him for ever. That he is here with me now gives me a constant reminder of what I might have lost – and how the innocent can be wrongly accused in the so-called name of justice . . .

Dave:

I have been through a long, eventful and often painful journey on and off the pitch. The 2008/09 football season has been traumatic enough. I don't need reminding of what has just happened at both Southampton and Stockport, two of my former clubs, who have come close to going out of existence. I was down in Southampton recently, at Eastleigh Town football club, for David Hughes' testimonial. As I walked in, fans slapped me on the back, asking me to go back. I appreciated that. Stockport gave me my first real opportunity in management, and Southampton gave me the chance to manage in the Premiership. They got every ounce of me and it's sad to see what both of them are going through. Thankfully I'm at a club that is going from strength to strength, a vital positive ingredient to take from the turmoil of what happened on that final, desperate May afternoon.

I wish the 2008/09 season had had a happy ending, but I will always be aware that this is, after all, only football. Yes I am passionate about it – and much more passionate than I might show publicly as I insist on retaining a cool, clear head as far as humanly possible – but this family has been through much worse. Since the court case I have experienced missing out through the play-offs at Wolves, winning promotion, suffering relegation, reaching the FA Cup final and now missing the play-offs again by one goal. It's been the classic sporting rollercoaster ride and I've been through every possible emotion along the way. But none of it compares to the emotion I felt the day I was accused of horrific child abuse and the day I walked free from court having successfully defended myself against those unbelievable charges. There is nothing that even comes close.

What those who sought to convict me of horrific child abuse did to me was take away something that I will never get back: my dignity. The whole experience felt like a dagger being continually stabbed through my heart. I can correct missing out on the play-offs because I am a fighter and that battling side will emerge again as I take Cardiff City forward. What I can never correct is the period of my life that was wrecked by the most horrific allegations any loving father could possibly face. At least now I have had the time to allow the raw wounds to heal and the opportunity to set the record straight, to tell my side of the most painful story imaginable.

Not making the play-offs is a horrible postscript and something none of us was expecting. But football was never the reason I wrote this book. For me to bear my soul and bring out all the issues that came up in my court case has drained me emotionally, but it's the right time to tell the world what I went through.

Hopefully this will represent closure for my family. But just as importantly, I want it to send out a message to those who think they can shout anything they like in the name of football banter. It's still happening to me and maybe I'll never stop it entirely, but I hope when people read this or hear about what I've been through they will realise what my family and I suffered together and ask themselves how they might have coped in the same dreadful circumstances.

It was actually only recently that we told our youngest, Georgia, what really happened all those years ago. She was simply too young in 1999, but now that she is in her mid-teens we had to let her know. She already had some idea because a few months ago she came screaming downstairs in floods of tears having read all this paedophile stuff put on the internet message boards by Swansea fans. We couldn't protect her any longer, so in the car on the way back from a Chinese takeaway, I took the plunge and told her what this book was really about; that it wasn't just football and that there may be parts of it that would hurt her. I told her that when she had finished reading it she'd know the full truth about what went on and the stories behind those cameramen being at the house when she was little – the ones she thought were there because Daddy had signed another player. I had wondered if telling her about the case would prove to be utterly traumatic, but fortunately she absorbed what I said and didn't over-react. That's got a lot to do with the relationship I have with my children, I think. We say it as we see it. Ann and I had often wondered how on earth we could broach the subject with her, but I felt so much better for finally doing it. It was cathartic, a final closure which hopefully will allow us to move on, bring success to Cardiff City and end a decade-long nightmare chapter in our lives.

I will be forever grateful to everyone who helped me and supported me throughout all the difficult times. Thankfully they are over. Now I am happy that I can say that I've seen yesterday, I am enjoying today and I am looking forward to tomorrow.